SELF-COMPASSIONATE MOTHERHOOD

3 Ways To Get You Out Of The Shadows Into The True Experience

CINDY CRANSWICK M.Phil, B.Couns

First published by Busybird Publishing 2018
Copyright © 2018 Cindy Cranswick

ISBN
Print: 978-1-925692-81-5
Ebook: 978-1-925692-82-2

Cindy Cranswick has asserted her right under the Copyright, Designs and Patents Act 1988 to be identified as the author of this work. The information in this book is based on the author's experiences and opinions. The publisher specifically disclaims responsibility for any adverse consequences, which may result from use of the information contained herein. Permission to use information has been sought by the author. Any breaches will be rectified in further editions of the book.

All rights reserved. No part of this publication may be reproduced, stored in or introduced into a retrieval system, or transmitted in any form, or by any means (electronic, mechanical, photocopying, recording or otherwise) without the prior written permission of the author. Any person who does any unauthorised act in relation to this publication may be liable to criminal prosecution and civil claims for damages. Enquiries should be made through the publisher.

Cover image: Dreamstime.com
Cover design: Busybird Publishing
Layout and typesetting: Busybird Publishing

Busybird Publishing
2/118 Para Road
Montmorency, Victoria
Australia 3094
www.busybird.com.au

This book is dedicated to all the mothers who have allowed me the privilege of sharing their journey through motherhood.

With much gratitude I share the knowledge and stories with you in the hope that motherhood becomes a more meaningful and joyful experience.

"Sometimes the strength of motherhood is greater than all natural laws."
– Barbara Kingsolver

Contents

Introduction	i
Chapter 1 – Identity Crisis	1
Chapter 2 – Motherhood Myths	11
Chapter 3 – Survival Blueprint	21
Chapter 4 – Be Selfish!	31
Chapter 5 – Shadow Self	41
Chapter 6 – True Self	49
Chapter 7 – Shadow Expectations	61
Chapter 8 – True Expectations	69
Chapter 9 – Shadow Emotions	77
Chapter 10 – True Emotions	85
Chapter 11 – Change Challenge	95
Chapter 12 – Meaningful Motherhood	107
Bibliography	119
About the Author	123
TLC – Therapeutic Lifestyle Changes	125

Introduction

Over the years I have watched far too many mothers lose the joy and meaning in their motherhood experience. It has made me look back on my own life and my own experiences of motherhood. I have realised that my mother's values of kindness and compassion have been an invaluable gift in my life. Her kindness and compassion provided me with the opportunity as a child to feel safe, loved and connected. This experience of secure attachment led me to believe that this was everyone's experience. Obviously, the reality is very different for many people. I became aware of how precious the gifts of kindness, compassion and secure attachment are in life.

When it came to my own experiences of motherhood with my two daughters, kindness and compassion were the strengths that got me through difficult times and allowed me to embrace the joy of being a mother. I believe my two daughters (now in their twenties) are my greatest achievement in life. They are kind, compassionate, amazing young women and I am so proud of them. I hope the gifts my mother gave me will be passed down for many generations to come.

In my early forties I had a mid-life crisis and decided to follow one of my dreams to become a counsellor. I gave up my career in the IT industry and went to university as a mature-aged student. This decision took me on a journey of personal discovery and allowed me the opportunity of truly understanding kindness and compassion through self-compassion. I realised the circle is not complete until *self* is brought into kindness and compassion. It changed my world and I began passing the gift on to my clients and others in my life.

Because of my own joyful and meaningful experience, I was curious about why so many mothers I encountered were not enjoying motherhood. Their experiences were shrouded in emotional suffering and distress. So, I decided to research why this was. My overall findings in the research were that mothers have an obvious lack of self-compassion and that self-compassion could be a source of prevention and treatment for emotional distress in the perinatal period. As a result of this, I ended up with a Master of Philosophy and a thesis that is sitting on my bookshelf.

Late last year I decided that I needed to write a book, as I doubted many mothers would ever end up reading my thesis. I needed to find a way to share my understanding of the challenges faced by mothers, to offer an opportunity for motherhood to be more meaningful and to bring more children into the world who feel safe, loved and connected. To share the gift of self-compassion with all mothers and their children.

This book is written for all the mothers, mothers-to-be and anyone who has an interest in meaningful motherhood experiences. It is my hope that through the understanding and practise of self-compassion, we can bring the joy and meaning back into this beautiful life experience of being a mother.

Chapter 1

Identity Crisis

"Motherhood: All love begins and ends there."
– Robert Browning

Becoming a mother is one of the most challenging, rewarding and soul-searching tasks in a woman's life. It has been described by many as the most unpredictable and joyous journey, and no two experiences are the same. It is also one of the most important times in your life when you will be required to create a new identity for yourself. Your arrival at this point may have been a long planned process or a sudden surprise but, whatever the reason, you are in for the ride of your life! There is no guide or perfect experience of motherhood. It is unique for each mother. Your journey will take its own course, no matter how many books you read, talks you attend or what you ask Dr Google. As you embark on this journey through motherhood, or if you have already begun, I would encourage you to read this book with an open, curious mind. Accept your own experience of motherhood as unique and your own identity as a mother as unique.

What does it mean to become a mother?

Anthropologists refer to the process of becoming a mother as "matrescence". It is a transition that has been overlooked and under-explored. Research in this life transition has mainly been focused on the development and outcomes for the baby and not on the exploration of the mother's experience. For many women, the transition to motherhood and the identity crisis that comes with it can have a significant impact on their well-being and mental health. It has been said that giving birth to a new identity as a mother can be as challenging as giving birth to a baby. In order to create an identity as a mother it would be useful to have a role description as to what this new identity may entail.

The meanings and definitions of what a mother is are virtually endless. A mother is a caregiver, a protector, a disciplinarian, a guide and a friend. A mother is a provider of safety, security and love who works tirelessly to make sure her children are equipped with the knowledge, values, skills and abilities to become competent human beings. Becoming a mother can be both the most joyful and the most challenging role a woman will undertake in life. From the day they arrive in this world, children will test your ability to be patient and, no matter what they do or say, as a mother you will always love them unconditionally. A mother is responsible for providing a safe and secure environment for her baby to grow and develop from the moment she conceives until the child becomes independent. I personally believe this continues way after independence, as a mother's role is never truly over – it is lifelong!

Being a mother means being there to teach your child important rules and roles in life, from being an empathetic human being to learning how to be responsible for their actions. A mother is a guide who helps her child to understand values in life as well as teach them the importance of an education, manners and more. A mother is also a disciplinarian who will model clear boundaries.

Someone who will teach their child the skills to respect others and themselves and to treat all people with empathy and compassion. There are many cultural definitions and descriptions of what it means to be a mother and it is useful for you to understand where your definition has come from.

We are not all fortunate enough to have had the experience of being mothered by the ideal mother – one that offers us unconditional love, safety, a sense of connectedness and a secure environment for us to develop to our full potential. This means many of us do not have good role models or an informed understanding of what it truly means to be a mother. For this reason, it is important for each of us to explore where our constructs of motherhood have come from and to question how this may influence our identity as mothers. If you haven't already explored this in detail this may be an opportunity for you to question what kind of mother you are or would like to be. Choose to create a unique identity for yourself as a mother that has meaning and purpose and one that is not modelled on past experiences or societal constructs.

Lost Identity

Over the years as a counsellor I have walked with many women through their motherhood journey. I have noticed some common challenges that directly impact their experience of motherhood and cause high levels of anxiety, depression and emotional distress. One of the major causes of emotional and psychological suffering in this transition to motherhood is the loss of identity. I have often heard mums say they "lost" their identity when they became a mother. However, it is more likely that they faced an identity crisis and they forgot to recreate their identity. Although we recreate or reconstruct our identity many times in life – from child to adolescent, from adolescent to adult, from student to employee, from being single to being in a relationship or after a significant loss – becoming a mother is often the most challenging recreation of identity. It requires the acceptance of a new identity and an adjustment and transition into becoming this person. Some of the challenges faced in creating and accepting this new identity have been identified as a loss of independence, social identity, and physical self. For mothers, this often results in decreased self-esteem, feelings of negative self-worth, increased levels of self-criticism and judgement. These negative views cause a high level of emotional distress that can lead to anxiety and depression and impacts negatively on the motherhood experience.

Accepting this new identity is a crucial element in a meaningful motherhood experience. Therefore, I thought it would be useful to explore how to make this shift into an acceptance of this new identity easier and more enjoyable. There are three main shifts we need to make to adjust to this new role and they are: Identity Shift, Your Unique Shift and the Emotional Shift.

Identity Shift

We all have the ability to make an identity shift and, as I mentioned, we have done it many times before without even realising that it takes strength, courage and skill to do so.

Think back to some of your identity shifts in life – what were the challenges you had recreating your identity? What strengths did you use to overcome the challenges? Perhaps some identity shifts you have made have been easier than others – why? Perhaps the shift from being single to married or in a relationship seemed easier than other shifts. Is this because you had time to plan and think about what it would be like before you committed to it?

Recreating our identity and making an identity shift can be a relatively easy task or it may be incredibly challenging. The ease of transition depends on a number of factors, including our own internal resources (emotional, psychological) and our external resources (support systems). Although we often plan our pregnancies I doubt many of us actually consider or plan for the identity shift and how we will transition into the new identity of a mother. I believe this is partly due to the societal view that becoming a mother is a natural transition in life. Although we are led to believe it is the most natural transition, as one of my clients stated, motherhood can be *"the most unnatural, unexpected experience"*.

We all know it is easier to accept change if you have prepared yourself for the change and you are committed to the change. Leaving it to the universe and hoping for the best might seem like a less stressful option but there is nothing more empowering than feeling like you have a choice! Choose to be prepared for the identity shift and, if you have already become a mother, notice how you have embraced the new identity. There may be parts of this new identity you still need to reconstruct or accept so that you can fully make the shift. The identity you had before becoming a mother has changed and this new identity as a mother holds a sense of meaning and purpose for both you and your child.

Your Unique Shift

Your shift will be unique! No two mothers will experience the same identity shift or embrace the new identity in the same way. There is no manual of a right or wrong way to make the transition into becoming a mother. Our maternal identity is often shaped by our own experience of being mothered or cared for as a child, but we still need to be aware of what that identity is made up of. We also need to be aware of the fact that not all our experiences of being mothered or cared for may have been how we want to mother and care for our children. We need to be prepared to create our own unique identity for ourselves as mothers. Having a baby is an act of creation. It is not only about the creation of a new life, it also requires the creation of a new identity for you as a mother.

Your personal experience of this will depend on many factors, including your personality, your family of origin, your views on life and motherhood, your support structure, your expectations, your strengths and weaknesses and your attitude. You know yourself better than anyone else and if you are honest with yourself you will be able to identify the challenges that might come up as you make your unique shift into motherhood. Remember it is unique, you are unique, and your child is unique – trust your intuition and step into your own unique experience of being a mum.

Emotional Shift

Be prepared for the emotional shift that comes with this new identity. The reason becoming a mother is considered one of the most challenging transitions in life is because it is also one of the most emotional transitions in life. The vast array of emotions from joy and happiness to sadness and fear make this journey not only incredibly rewarding but also incredibly challenging. The combination of hormones, emotions and sleep deprivation often catch mothers by surprise and increase their levels of emotional distress.

Current statistics show that one in five Australian mothers suffer from perinatal (pre- and post-natal) anxiety and or depression (PANDA, 2017). There are many more who are not diagnosed who also experience high levels of emotional distress. Whilst most mothers are prepared for the practical aspects of becoming a mother, they are very unprepared for the emotional rollercoaster they are about to embark on. There is very little psycho-education given to mothers and very few skills taught on how to deal with making the emotional shift into motherhood. Many mothers who experience anxiety and/or depression in the perinatal period say that it does not feel like the depression or anxiety that they have experienced at other times in life. This has now been validated by the latest findings in neuroscience. These findings have identified that a woman's brain is structurally and functionally different in the perinatal period (from conception to up to three years after birth). The symptoms and presentation of anxiety and depression are also different. This may be attributed to the influence of the caregiving system that is activated in motherhood (Pawluski, Lonstein & Fleming, 2017). It could also explain why some mothers report that one day (often around the time a child turns three) it just "stopped" the depression or anxiety just "turned off", or it's as though someone just "flicked a switch".

Not all mothers will experience anxiety and/or depression in the perinatal period, but they will experience difficult emotions. Having the skills to accept these difficult emotions as part of the experience is an essential element in making motherhood meaningful and enjoyable. Preparing for the emotional shift into the new identity of a mother is not addressed well enough in our society. I will be focusing on this topic in more detail later in this book. For now, I would like you to think of how you have dealt with difficult emotions in the past and whether or not this has been helpful for you.

Making the Shift

To help illustrate the importance of recreating your identity and making the shifts, I thought it might be useful to tell you Sarah's story.

Sarah came to see me for counselling after she was diagnosed with perinatal anxiety. Her baby was three months old and Sarah was not coping very well. Her baby was healthy and apart from not being the best sleeper at night she was a delight. Sarah had a relatively easy birth and was still breastfeeding. She was happily married, had family support from her parents and her partner's parents. She had not experienced anxiety before and was feeling overwhelmed and out of control when it took over.

Before having her baby, Sarah was a very successful career woman, working in a mainly male-dominated field. She loved her job and was well respected by her colleagues. Sarah and her partner had planned for their baby and although she was enjoying motherhood it was not what she expected it to be. She was not prepared for all the unproductive time, the feelings of intense 24/7 responsibilities or the array of emotions. She also found herself crying a lot and feeling isolated. She thought perhaps she was depressed too.

After a few sessions with Sarah it became very obvious that she had not prepared herself for the transition (the shifts) to her new identity as a mother. She had the view that motherhood would come naturally. It seemed to have been so natural for her sister and for her friends. She felt guilty that she was not really enjoying it and that she didn't really feel like she was qualified to be a mum. Sarah's meaningful identity that she felt comfortable in was her identity as a career woman. This new identity as a mother was unknown and did not have the levels of productivity and achievement she was accustomed to. Sarah worked back through the three shifts.

Her identity shift – Who was she now? What strengths and values was she able to draw on in this new identity? What parts of the career identity would be useful to integrate into her identity as a mother?

Her unique shift – What kind of mother would she like to be? Why was it so important for her to be that kind of mother? How would her identity as a mother be different and have meaning for her?

Her emotional shift – How was she going to deal with her emotions? What strategies had she used in the past to comfort herself when she experienced difficult emotions? How could she make her baby feel loved and connected to her?

By working through the shifts, Sarah created a unique identity for herself as a mother that had meaning and purpose. With the anxiety that she was experiencing reduced to a manageable level, she was no longer worried about who she was supposed to be, how she was supposed to be doing things and whether or not she was being productive. Sarah was able to step into her unique identity as a mother and embrace the experience. She also knew that in the not-too-distant future she would need to do the process all over again as she stepped into the combined identity of career woman and mother.

Meaning Making

Once we construct an identity that has meaning and purpose we have the ability to alleviate emotional distress. The concept of meaning making has its roots in the earliest forms of psychological therapies. These meaning making therapies place a lot of emphasis on the need to recreate and make sense of our identity whenever there is a change in our life's course.

Over the years research has shown that having meaningful experiences in life is what creates a sense of happiness and makes life worth living. If we find meaning in life's experiences we tend to have improved mental health, self-worth, and self-confidence. If we have a sense of purpose and know what we are living for then we tend to feel good about who we are and what we are doing. Making meaning is also a form of story-telling. We are the main character in our story and it is the story we tell ourselves that determines what meaning we make of our life experiences. What story are you writing or have you written about your experience of motherhood? Have you included your new identity in your story?

Preparing for, recreating and accepting your new identity as a mother is an essential part of ensuring your experience is unique and meaningful. Please take the time to create an identity that you can relate to, an identity that gives you a sense of purpose and meaning as a mother and allows you to fully embrace this amazing life experience.

Chapter 2

Motherhood Myths

"There's no way to be a perfect mother and a
million ways to be a good one."
– Jill Churchill

Over the years, many myths have been told about motherhood and the experience of becoming a mother. These myths have created a collective confusion that has been accelerated with the social media movement. I believe this Mythological Motherhood phenomenon has created a gap between the expectations mothers have of themselves and the reality they experience.

What is a myth?
A simple definition of a myth is a story handed down through history that explains and gives value to the unknown and helps us make sense of how we experience the world. Another definition of a myth is a widely held but false belief or idea. Historically, myths have been viewed as a source of spiritual growth and understanding. There are

many myths that have helped us as humans make sense of experiences and events and learn from others stories of the past to enable us to be more prepared for the future.

There is a common view that many myths are just stories that hold no valid truth and cause more angst than growth. Most of the myths of motherhood fall into the category of falsehood and more often than not cause our views and expectations of motherhood to be unrealistic. This results in unnecessary worry, fear and distress.

If we buy into these myths the expectations, pressure and judgement we place on ourselves as mothers can become overwhelming. There are many myths surrounding the motherhood experience that influence how mothers judge themselves and create expectations not only for themselves, but also for their babies. In this chapter, I thought it would be useful to discuss some of the most common, unhelpful myths that have been created around motherhood in today's society.

Myth 1
Motherhood is natural, easy and instinctive. The first part of this myth – natural – implies that as mothers we know exactly what to do, how to do it and that we are naturally designed and wired to be mothers. The second part – easy – is probably the biggest lie any woman could ever be led to believe! The third part – instinctive – again implies that we should instinctually know what to expect and what to do and how to do it.

Reality 1
The reality is that motherhood does not always feel like a natural process and many aspects of being a mother feel very unnatural. Being pregnant does not feel natural for many women but they don't admit it for fear of being judged. If they believe this myth then they are constantly questioning why pregnancy does not feel natural to them and what is wrong with them. The same goes for giving

birth and breastfeeding – these two tasks of motherhood again do not come naturally for many women and are often the source of extreme distress.

There is no doubt that motherhood is not easy – it is one of the most challenging tasks in life. Promoting the assumption that it is easy is setting mothers up to question their skills and capabilities, again causing unnecessary feelings of being overwhelmed at the complexities of the task. As we are all born with a natural care-giving system there are parts of motherhood that perhaps are instinctual, but as we all know listening to instinct and intuition is not something that we do well as humans. Rather than following our instinct and intuition we tend to follow stereotypes and other people's expectations. Our fear of failure often interferes with our ability to follow our instinctual insights.

Myth 2
There is a right way to mother. This myth leads to the unrealistic assumption that there is a guide or manual out there to follow and abide by that will produce securely attached, well-behaved children. It also implies that if you do it the *wrong way* you will need to be accountable to all of those mothers who have done it the right way and you will be forever judged for not following the manual! This myth not only divides us, but it also encourages us not to trust our own intuition and instead conform to a set of rules and guidelines.

Reality 2
The right way for you is as unique as the one-of-a-kind connection you share with your child. The reality is there is no right or wrong way to mother your children and often the strategies and techniques you use with one child will not be the same for another child. Yes, there are some basic common sense skills, but there is certainly no right or wrong way of applying these skills. There are so many mothers out there who are second-guessing every move they make and every day they spend with their children for the fear

of being judged as a "bad" mother who got it all wrong! Although research has come a long way toward helping us understand the needs of children, the experience for mothers to thrive requires a greater emphasis on and respect for our biological instincts and innate wisdom. The answer is to mother your way!

Myth 3

A good mother can do it all. Firstly, the emphasis in this myth on the concept of a "good mother" needs to be questioned! A good mother seems to be an almost unachievable label for most mothers I have come across in my counselling work. The goal post is constantly moved as to what this definition of a "good mother" really is making it an elusive goal that is impossible to attain. A "good enough" mother would be more appropriate terminology to refer to and for mothers to aspire to. The "can do it all" aspect of this myth implies that mothers are potentially super-humans who have the ability to do many different tasks at once, be in many different places at once and meet the needs of many different people at the same time!

Reality 3

The reality is: *"Good enough mothers can perform the most amazing balancing acts"*. Motherhood is more like a juggling act than a balancing act. The quicker you become used to the fact that you will be unbalanced a lot of the time in your motherhood experience the sooner you will become more accepting of this circus act.

Yes, mothers can do a lot and can multi-task better than most people. However, the expectation that mothers can do it all is completely unrealistic and causes many mothers to exhaust themselves in their motherhood journey. They try to do too much in order to meet this unrealistic expectation. Many mothers have mentioned to me that they just need to find a balance then they will be able to do it all! Attempting to hold a balance at any time in your life (for more than a few minutes) is like holding a handstand for any real length of time. It's not only exhausting, but it requires so much focus that you end up missing out on the richness all around you. I much prefer the concept of being mindful and in the present moment. Once we have the ability to be mindful we find a sense of centredness. We can connect to a powerful, peaceful place within, even though the world around us seems imbalanced. Later in this book we will discuss some ways to become more mindful and find your peaceful place within.

Myth 4

Asking for help is a sign of weakness. There is a common belief out there in Western cultures that we can get through life on our own – that we don't need anyone's help and, more often than not, asking for help is seen as a sign of weakness. This myth in motherhood is driven by the assumption that we should know what to do and how to do it. If we ask for help we may be viewed as failures or "not good enough mothers".

This myth and other similar unhelpful beliefs have resulted in mothers becoming more and more isolated and feeling more and more overwhelmed by the solitary responsibility of raising a child.

Reality 4

The reality is we aren't meant to raise children alone. The notion of "independence" that so many mothers feel they must maintain is yet another product of a society still working out what freedom actually is. Because oppression is so often associated with dependency we've forgotten our basic human need for interdependency and inadvertently glamorised isolation. This social isolation is responsible for and is one of the many causes of anxiety, depression and distress in the perinatal period. In community-based cultures there is no need to have to ask for help when raising a child. It is just part of the beliefs and values of those cultures that everyone who is in any way connected to the child will be available to help the mother and the child at any time.

There is a sense of respect and genuine positive regard for mothers who accept the help. Their cultural belief is that no one person can raise a child successfully and, as the African proverb goes, *"It takes a village to raise a child"*. The literal meaning is that it takes an entire community of different people interacting with children in order for children to experience and grow in a safe environment.

Myth 5

You should be enjoying every moment. This is a myth that mothers have told me rings through their ears on a daily basis. It is the source of a lot of unnecessary guilt and emotional pain. It's a bit like saying we should enjoy every moment in life – although many of us strive to do this, it is an almost impossible task to achieve. Once again, a myth that sets mothers up to fail, to judge and be judged!

Reality 5

The reality is I doubt there is any mother who could honestly say they enjoyed "every" moment of being a mother. People who say this to you likely either suffer from a great deal of guilt themselves or they have selective memory regarding their own motherhood experiences. Mostly people who say this to you are not trying to make you feel guilty or judge you. They are merely trying to connect with you and they are referring to the whole motherhood experience being a joyful memory. What they are forgetting is that there are many moments in motherhood that are painful, challenging and even overwhelming. The brain has the most incredible ability to filter out those moments and remind you only of the joyful motherhood moments. I believe that this is the finest demonstration of selective memory and demonstrates how love and connectedness can heal painful wounds and memories.

Myth 6
Your inadequacies are the reasons for the frustration you feel. This myth implies that our flaws, weaknesses and lack of skill play a role in the frustrations we may feel in our experience of motherhood. Although these flaws, weaknesses and lack of skills may have been with us throughout our lives, for some reason in the motherhood experience, this myth allows them to be front and centre stage for the reason why we feel frustrated.

Reality 6
No one is perfect and we all have flaws, weaknesses and lack certain skills and these do cause us frustration throughout life. But the reality is in motherhood the majority of the frustration we feel in this regard is related to setting ourselves unrealistic expectations. Instead of accepting who we are, what our capabilities are and what our strengths are, we focus on unrealistic expectations that we will never achieve. The gap between unrealistic expectations and reality has to be filled. In motherhood that gap is often filled with emotional suffering in the form of frustration, anger, guilt, anxiety and depression. Learning the art of self-acceptance and self-kindness in motherhood will allow us to be more realistic in our expectations.

Myth 7
Guilt is the price you must pay for the love you experience. The acceptance of feeling guilty in motherhood has become an acceptable norm. I am constantly taken aback at how many women tell me they are consumed with guilt but have come to accept it as part of the experience of becoming a mother. Guilt is an emotion that we experience throughout life not just during our motherhood experience. It is an emotion driven by the belief that we have caused harm, done something wrong or compromised our values.

Reality 7
Guilt is often one of the many prices we pay for judgemental, unchecked thoughts. The constant comparisons mothers subject themselves to encourages the justification of guilt. Today's mothers are constantly comparing themselves to constructs and expectations of motherhood that they see in the media, in friendship groups or mothers groups. Trying to live up to family beliefs or expectations that have passed down through the generations can cause us to go against our own values, which results in unnecessary and often overwhelming feelings of guilt. The reality is that there is no need for guilt in the motherhood experience and the deeper our self-awareness, self-love and self-respect, the less power such draining emotions have over our lives.

Myth 8
If everything is organised mothering will be joyful. This myth implies that organisation is the source of a joyful life. This leads to mothers exhausting themselves trying to make sure that everything in their lives is organised and controlled.

Reality 8
The reality is that we will experience more joy in our motherhood experience when we let go of the perception that organising our external environment is the answer to our internal sense of peace and joy. Rather than focusing on organising our external world we should be focusing on organising our internal world. By doing this we allow for more clarity of mind and as a result the world around us will seem more organised.

Myth 9
Stay-at-home mums lack intelligence, motivation, or competency. Sadly, this is a myth that still haunts many women in our society today. With the rise in women becoming more independent and playing a significant role in the workforce this myth causes a lot of unnecessary distress and suffering.

Reality 9

Freedom of choice is still such a new reality for women in today's society and the choice to stay home has been unjustly associated with the very oppression we have fought so hard to escape. It is important that we don't settle for the opposite extreme and stigmatise stay-at-home mothers. We need to encourage and support each mother's intuition and integrity to decide what is best for her child and her family. This is the true indicator of freedom of choice. The reality is that stay-at-home mothers are intelligent, highly motivated and competent women who understand the significance of the first three years of a child's life. They believe their role as stay-at-home mothers is of significant value to our society.

Myth 10

Working mums love their children less and do not have strong attachments with them. This myth and the previous one go hand-in-hand and it's a bit like you are damned if you do or damned if you don't. Pressures and judgements placed on women who choose to return to work and full-time employment results in feelings of guilt around the fears of attachment, bonding and wellbeing of their children. They often present with high levels of anxiety as they try to reconcile their choice with the expectation of others.

Reality 10

Some women's intuition leads them to the realisation that they need to continue working in order to *best* care for their children. Stigmatising mothers who work away from home is just as destructive and divisive as its opposite. Instead, we should choose to focus our attention on supporting the mother and child connection, whatever that means for each family. Social shifts such as benefits for part-time employees, longer maternity leave, workplace childcare and community building initiatives are a much more empowering place to focus our energy.

The "motherhood rule wars" are weakening our ability to determine and create what we really want and need as mothers. Secure attachment can be achieved regardless of whether or not you are with your child all day or for limited periods during the day. We will explore attachment in more detail later in this book.

These are only some of the myths mothers are subjected to on a regular basis but believe me there are many more. I haven't even touched on the myths around birthing, breastfeeding, bonding and attachment, developmental milestones, mothers body image and relationships. I could probably write a book on myths alone! So, as this chapter comes to an end, perhaps this would be a good time to reflect on some of the myths that may have influenced or be influencing your experience of motherhood and question the value of these mythical stories.

Chapter 3

Survival Blueprint

"Mother love in infancy and childhood are as important for mental health as are vitamins and protein for physical health."
– John Bowlby

I could not write a book on motherhood without devoting a chapter to the importance of attachment in your experience as a mother and caregiver. Working not only with mothers but also with all my clients, I have seen the impact and importance of each of us having an informed and educated understanding of our own attachment style or survival blueprint.

Our early experiences of attachment with our primary caregiver create our blueprint for survival – it determines how we thrive and survive in the world. Mothers are usually the primary caregivers and it is vitally important for us to understand the influence we have on our children's attachment style.

What is attachment?

According to psychologist Mary Ainsworth, attachment *"may be defined as an affectional tie that one person or animal forms between himself and another specific one – a tie that binds them together in space and endures over time"*.

Today's mothers are increasingly aware of the importance of secure attachment for their child's development and wellbeing but there is not much education and information offered on how to achieve this. There is a lot of fear and expectation for mothers around the issue of bonding and attachment that often creates unnecessary anxiety. As a mother or mother-to-be it is important to understand your own attachment style and be aware of what is required for your baby to experience secure attachment. I truly believe that this is one of the greatest gifts you can give your child. Their future emotional wellbeing and ability to experience meaningful relationships depends on this.

John Bowlby recognised the importance of attachment and was the founder of the attachment theory. He stated that, *"Attachment is a lasting psychological connectedness between human beings"*. Attachment is an emotional bond – one of the earliest bonds formed by children with their caregivers in order to survive and thrive. Babies are born with the innate drive to form attachment with a caregiver – normally their mother – and in turn the mother's caregiving system is designed to offer attachment in the form of love, food, connection, comfort and physical touch. The caregiving system goes hand-in-hand with the attachment system.

So, what determines successful attachment? Bowlby and others found evidence that food alone did not determine secure attachment, but that being nurtured and receiving consistent responsiveness from the caregiver were the primary determinants of attachment. The main theme of attachment theory implies that if primary caregivers are available and responsive to their child's needs this allows the child to develop a sense of safety and security. The child comes to know that the caregiver is reliable and dependable, which creates a secure base for the child to then explore the world.

Why is attachment important?
Firstly, attachment helps keep infants and children close to their caregivers so that they can be protected and have more chance of survival. Secondly, the important emotional bond created through attachment also provides children with a secure base from which they can then safely explore their environment. Thirdly, as many researchers including Ainsworth, Bowlby, Main, and Solomon have identified, how a child is attached to his or her caregivers can have a major influence both during childhood and later in life. The failure to form a secure attachment with a caregiver has been linked to a number of childhood behavioural problems, including conduct disorder and oppositional-defiant disorder. Researchers also suggest that the type of attachment displayed early in life can have a lasting effect on adult relationships.

Attachment Styles
Depending on the consistency of the caregiving relationship, every child develops an attachment style or pattern as a result of this early emotional bond. There are four attachment styles that have been identified and they include secure attachment, avoidant attachment, ambivalent attachment and disorganised attachment.

Secure Attachment
This is the ideal attachment style needed to enjoy healthy boundaries, intimacy, independence and connection. This style is a result of a child having a caregiver who is attuned to them and provides safety, care, consistency, attention and affection. Children who experience this type of connection

grow to feel safe, to interact and trust others, explore the world around them and have emotional regulation and resilience. As adults they display greater self-confidence, have more meaningful relationships and have more emotional intelligence and wellbeing. Securely attached children are able to safely separate from their parent or caregiver and they seek comfort from their caregiver when they are frightened. There is evidence to say that securely attached children are more empathic, less aggressive and disruptive and often more mature than insecurely attached children.

Securely attached adults have trusting, lasting relationships, tend to have healthy levels of self-esteem, are comfortable sharing their feelings and they seek out support in times of need. Mothers of securely attached children tend to play more with their children, react and respond quicker to their children's needs and are generally more responsive to their children than parents of insecurely attached children. If our needs were met as children and we had the experience of feeling safe and loved, then as mothers we are more likely to be able to offer our children the experience of secure attachment.

Avoidant Attachment

Avoidant attachment style is a result of the caregiver not being emotionally available, being insensitive to the child's needs and sometimes offering hostile responses to the child's need for connection. This results in the child forming a coping strategy of disconnection. Most avoidant attached people find their greatest struggle is a lack of emotion. If we are not nurtured from a young age part of our brain called the limbic system is neurologically starved and does not receive the signals to build social responses needed for emotional bonding and connection. This disconnection from the caregiver results in disconnection from relationships in the future and leads to isolation.

Avoidant attached children do not seek as much comfort or contact from their caregivers; they show little preference for caregivers over strangers and may often avoid their caregiver. The avoidance is more obvious when there has been a period of absence or separation from the caregiver. As adults, those with an avoidant attachment tend to have difficulty with connection, intimacy and close relationships. People with avoidant attachment find it difficult to express their emotions and they do not invest much emotional connection in their relationships. They also experience lower levels of distress when a relationship ends. They often avoid intimacy by using irrelevant or irrational excuses.

Other common characteristics include a failure to support partners during stressful times and an inability to share feelings, thoughts, and emotions with partners.

Ambivalent Attachment

When a caregiver is on again, off again – connected and then disconnected, attentive then inattentive – this results in ambivalent or anxious attachment. The lack of consistency causes doubt as to whether the child's needs will be met. The child becomes hypervigilant, looking out for cues as to how their behaviour might influence the caregiver's response so they can get what they need. Over time they find themselves on an emotional see-saw of needs being met and not being met. They create a script or rule that says, "*I can want, but cannot have*".

Ambivalent attached people often display high levels of dissatisfaction with life and in relationships. If others do become emotionally available to them they will become unavailable and model the treatment they received when they were trying to get their needs met. Children who are ambivalently attached tend to be extremely suspicious of strangers. These children display considerable distress when separated from a parent or caregiver, but do not seem reassured or comforted by the return of the parent. In some cases, the child might passively reject the parent by refusing comfort or may openly display direct aggression toward the parent. Ambivalent attachment has a direct link to the lack of availability of a mother or significant caregiver. These children are often described as clingy or needy and over-dependent. As adults, those with an ambivalent attachment style often have difficulty in allowing themselves to get close to others as they fear they will be rejected and that their partner will not reciprocate their affection. This often results in frequent breakups and the relationship feels distant and disconnected.

Some ambivalently attached adults have the tendency to cling to young children in order to feel safe, loved and connected. This can be misinterpreted as smothering or being too full on.

Disorganised Attachment

A disorganised attachment style results when the caregiver presents mixed messages to the child. This is like a push and pull effect – *"Come here, go away"*. Parents create situations for the child that are unsolvable and unwinnable. This type of connection creates confusion and fear for the child who in turn needs to disconnect from the caregiver.

The disorganised pattern arises in the child when there is a desire to be close to the parent as an object of safety, conflicting with a drive to detach from a dangerous and confusing caregiver. For the adult this may mean being held emotionally hostage by the conflict of the desire for intimacy, as well as the fear of it. Children with a disorganised insecure attachment style demonstrate a mixture of behaviours including resistance and avoidance. They can sometimes present confused or dazed and are often apprehensive in the presence of their caregiver. The inconsistency they received from their caregiver is a major factor in this style of attachment. If the caregiver is both the source of fear for a child and the source of reassurance there is good reason for confusion to arise and for the result to be a disorganised attachment style.

Adults with disorganised attachment styles find it difficult to be in relationship and are often unable to sustain long-term meaningful relationships.

What is your attachment style?

It is not common for us to ask someone what their attachment style is. We feel far more comfortable asking people what their zodiac star sign is than asking the difficult and often unknown question of attachment. Yet our attachment styles are not only a predictor of a meaningful motherhood relationship but also one of the most accurate predictors of meaningful intimate relationships. The fact is 50% of us have a secure attachment style, 20% of us have an ambivalent attachment style, 25% have an avoidant attachment style and 3-5% have a disorganised attachment style (Levine & Heller, 2012). The good news is that regardless of our attachment style we are able to learn to be securely attached and in turn are able to offer our children and those we are in relationship with a secure attachment experience.

Dr Diane Poole Heller is a renowned expert in the field of adult attachment and she has undertaken valuable research in the area of repairing adult attachment. If you are not aware of your attachment style, now is as good a time as any to find out. There are many adult attachment questionnaires available online that will give you an accurate indication of your attachment style.

Remember: regardless of your attachment style you can learn to be securely attached and you can have securely attached children. This was confirmed in a recent article by Dan Siegel and Alan Sroufe, who stated that, *"It is possible to develop a secure attachment state of mind as an adult – even in the face of a difficult childhood"*. As we know from neuroscience, the brain continues to remodel itself in response to experiences throughout our lives. This means that through positive experiences of feeling safe, nurtured, loved and accepted we can repair attachment ruptures.

What influences the development of secure attachment?

I have highlighted above some of the factors that lead to the insecure styles of attachment, but regardless of your own attachment style as a mother there are some simple factors that you can put into practice now that will make a difference to your child's experience of attachment.

These factors are:

- Maternal warmth – the ability to show care and compassion in a consistent and regular way to offer a sense of safety.

- Reflective mindful parenting – the ability to be tuned into (connected) and fully focused on the needs of your child.

- Avoiding unstable environments – these cause fear and anxiety to you as the caregiver and will directly impact your child causing heightened levels of fear and anxiety and feelings of being unsafe.

- Reducing your child's exposure to stress and trauma – this causes your child's safety and threat system to be on high alert and has long-term developmental consequences as toxic stress interferes with healthy brain development.

This might all sound rather complex and difficult to put into action but as we journey through this book I will offer you some key skills that will help you achieve this focused attunement and attachment with your child.

In closing this chapter, I would like to share a story with you on how some of the most basic actions can make a child feel safe and secure. There was an aid worker who had an interest in attachment and was hoping to make a difference to the lives of mothers and children. Her goal seemed futile as the war conditions created an environment of stress, fear and trauma – not only for the mothers but also for all of their children.

Although she could not offer them ways to achieve the steps above to try and offer their children a secure attachment experience, she decided to take it right back to the simple basics of what is needed for a child to feel loved, nurtured and safe. She printed labels on the loaves of bread that were being distributed by aid organisations and on it were three simple instructions:

> Hug your child every day
>
> Take care of yourself (sleep more)
>
> Make eye contact with your child

It sounds so simple, but you would be surprised at how many mothers in today's society have missed the three basic steps of connection and safety. Our earliest form of communication is through body language and eye contact. You will notice that babies are constantly seeking out contact with others through their eyes. They read signs of safety and danger from what they sense around them. We live in a society that is driven by technology and, although there are many advantages to the technological boom, we have lost sight of some of the most basic forms of human connection.

I am constantly saddened when I see mothers or parents out with their children on their mobile phones. They are connected to the virtual world and completely disconnected from their beautiful babies and children who are desperate for their attention. There are so many developmental and attachment issues that could be solved for our children if we would all just take the time to make eye contact with them.

Truly connect with them and let them be seen – as they said in the movie *Avatar*: "*I see you*". The power of those three words is not to be underestimated. Please see your child, hug your child and truly feel the connection, as there is no greater feeling than to be truly seen.

Chapter 4

Be Selfish!

"If your compassion does not include yourself, it is incomplete."
– Jack Kornfield

When I introduce the concept of self-compassion to people their response is often, *"But I have always been told to put others first and not to be selfish!"* The reality is quite the opposite. If we are kind and compassionate to ourselves we are more likely to be kind, compassionate and understanding to others and more likely to feel connected to others. We are led to believe that there is always someone out there who is worse off than we are – perhaps our cultural views and beliefs are responsible for this notion that we should put others before ourselves. Dr Kristin Neff (2012) defines self-compassion as *"extending compassion to one's self in times of perceived inadequacy, failure or general suffering"*.

Before you judge the concept of self-compassion and come up with resistance to it, I invite you to be open and curious as you read this chapter. Perhaps after gaining an understanding of the importance of self-compassion not only for yourself, but also for your relationships with your children and other significant people in your life, you may join me in my quest to create a self-compassionate society where people live meaningful lives.

In order to understand the concept of self-compassion there is a need to define and understand compassion. The standard definition of compassion, according to Paul Gilbert (2009), is *"a sensitivity to suffering in self and others with a commitment to try and alleviate and prevent it"*. Compassion literally means to *"suffer with"*. Think about what it is like to show compassion to another person that you care about. You will notice that you firstly see their pain and then feel a warmth and desire to alleviate their pain or suffering. You will also be inclined to show them kindness and understanding in times of failure rather than judging or criticising them. You will also probably notice that you accept that they are not perfect and that their failures and mistakes are just part of being human.

In Buddhism, compassion is seen as a way to help people train their minds in order to improve wellbeing and foster enlightenment. The compassionate view of themselves and others that an individual develops enables them to cope with difficult emotions and challenges with greater awareness and understanding. The value of compassion on our emotional, psychological and physical health has been the subject of many research studies over the last twenty-five years. As a result of this the construct of compassion has been broken down into three main areas: compassion we experience for others, compassion we experience from others and self-compassion.

In the last decade, self-compassion has become an area of significant interest and research in psychology. Self-compassion is the ability to act the same way towards ourselves as we would to others we care about when we are having a hard time, when we are suffering or when we fail. Instead of ignoring our pain, self-compassion allows us to comfort and care for ourselves and acknowledge how difficult it is. Instead of criticising and judging ourselves when we fail, we can offer kindness, understanding and the acceptance that being human means we are not perfect. Self-compassion helps us develop a healthy and caring attitude towards ourselves and is an important factor in the development of our own psychological wellbeing. We are born with the innate ability to be compassionate and caring to others and ourselves, but somewhere along the way and for many different reasons we are taught to focus on others and not take care of ourselves. People who are raised in safe, secure environments who experience validating relationships with caregivers may be more likely to relate to others and themselves in a compassionate and caring way.

After working for many years with my clients and using self-compassion to underpin my counselling work, I embarked on a research project to identify if a lack of self-compassion in motherhood could be a predictor of anxiety, depression and distress in the perinatal period. My findings from this research have resulted in the book you are now reading.

What is self-compassion?
Dr Kristin Neff, the guru of self-compassion, has defined self-compassion as consisting of three main elements: self-kindness, common humanity and mindfulness (Neff, 2011).

- *Self-kindness* is described as the ability to show kindness to oneself instead of criticism, self-doubt and judgement. Self-kindness is also the act of being gentle when confronted with painful experiences and being able to comfort and soothe ourselves.

- *Common humanity* is the acceptance and understanding of the shared human experience (not unique to self), including acceptance of suffering in the face of failure and the ability to deal with unmet expectations with compassion and understanding.

- *Mindfulness* is a way of acceptance when experiencing painful feelings and thoughts instead of over-identifying with them and being able to hold them in awareness. Mindfulness fosters a flexible thought process that is not influenced by personal views but allows for a non-judgemental acceptance of feelings and mental states.

Self-compassion and emotional wellbeing

There is a lot of research that consistently suggests that greater self-compassion is an important source of wellbeing and is associated with reduced negative states of mind such as anxiety, depression and stress. One study found an association between self-compassion and lower levels of depression and showed evidence for the relationship between self-compassion and mental health. It demonstrated that higher levels of self-compassion were associated with lower levels of mental health symptoms. The key features of self-compassion highlighted in this study were the lack of self-criticism and self-doubt, which are known to be important predictors in the development of anxiety and depression. This shows us the importance of self-compassion in developing wellbeing, reducing depression and anxiety, and increasing resilience to stress (Neff & Costigan, 2014).

Self-compassion has also been linked to less perfectionism, rumination (over-thinking), and fear of failure. It encourages higher levels of resilience and helps us reduce our reactions to negative events. People with higher levels of self-compassion have more accepting thoughts, less negative emotions and a greater ability to acknowledge responsibility and put their negative experiences into perspective. Self-compassionate people do not get rid of or ignore negative emotions, they accept and validate the importance of their emotions, and have the ability to self-soothe and take care of themselves in times of suffering or failure. It has been suggested that self-compassion is associated with a number of psychological strengths and resilience. People who are more self-compassionate report feeling happier than those who lack self-compassion. Self-compassionate people display higher levels of gratitude, curiosity, emotional intelligence, initiative, optimism, connectedness, intellectual flexibility, and life satisfaction (Neff, Hsieh & Dejitterat, 2005).

How do we become self-compassionate?

The good news is that self-compassion is not just a pre-existing personality trait, but a skill that can be acquired through education, training and psychological interventions (Smeets, Neff, Alberts, & Peters, 2014; Shapira & Mongrain, 2010). Being kind and empathic to others is a trait that exists in all of us and compassion is a learnt response to the pain and suffering of others. Self-compassion is a skill that can be learnt. The development of self-compassion has a direct impact on our psychological wellbeing. It is an essential component of living a meaningful life and adapting to transitions in life.

We know that a mother's psychological state directly affects the child's wellbeing and influences the development of a secure attachment. If we experience maternal anxiety and/or depression, our caregiving behaviour can be impacted. Our ability to be sensitive and supportive of our child's needs may be influenced by our own needs. It has been suggested that self-compassion is a pre-requisite for healthy, secure attachment and good parenting. Self-compassion is critical to the development of compassion for others and Goldstein (2003) has described it as *"the heartfelt experience of sharing the pain of another and the wish for alleviation of their suffering"*. Mothers who are self-compassionate are more able to perceive their child's distress, separate from their own distress, and respond appropriately. The common humanity element of self-compassion, as defined by Neff (2011), reduces self-judgement and shifts self-blame in mothering and allows attention to be focused on the present tasks. As mothers with depression tend to over-think and become absorbed in self-blame and criticism, this could prove to be an essential element in the development of secure attachment. The mindfulness element of self-compassion allows a mother to have greater awareness of their child's needs and enables them to respond sensitively.

Through self-compassion, a mother is able to devote kindness and acceptance towards herself and show the same kindness and acceptance to their child, especially in negative emotional situations. It has been said that self-compassion is particularly useful for a mother's mental health issues, such as anxiety and depression.

A mother who is able to pay compassionate attention to their child may be able to connect to positive feelings and view themselves and their relationship with their child more positively. Therefore, a mother with self-compassion will be in a more mindful state and may be less likely to over-identify with emotions, will be more accepting of external or situational causes of behavior that are common to all human experience, and be able to tolerate negative emotions through the ability to self-soothe (Cranswick, 2017).

The research on self-compassion offers strong evidence that it is a valuable coping resource when people experience major life stressors, negative life events or developmental transitions. Self-compassionate people are less likely to catastrophise negative life experiences, experience anxiety or depression after major life stressors, and avoid challenging tasks for fear of failure. Self-compassion can play an important role in the human coping experience.

With all this evidence on the importance of self-compassion I am still surprised at the resistance we all have in being kind and caring towards ourselves!

What self-compassion is not!

Self-pity

When we become immersed in self-pity we only focus on our own problems and seem to forget that others have problems, too. There is this assumption that no one else is experiencing the same issues and we tend to isolate ourselves from others and exaggerate the pain and suffering the problem is causing us.

Self-compassion, on the other hand, allows us to notice that others are also experiencing problems (often similar to ours) and gives us the ability to reach out and connect instead of disconnecting and isolating ourselves. When we give in to self-pity we allow ourselves to be caught up in emotional drama. We lack the ability to bring logic and reasoning into the experience. Self-compassion allows us to put our problems into perspective, to see the bigger picture and regulate our difficult emotions.

Self-indulgence

I have heard many people saying that they are fearful to be self-compassionate as this might lead them to believe that they can do anything they like and get away with it. For example, after a hard day at work I may decide that being kind to myself means eating a tub of ice cream or drinking a bottle of wine or watching eight hours of my favourite Netflix series all in one sitting! These are typical examples of self-indulgence, not self-compassion.

Self-compassion or being compassionate to yourself means that you want to care for and nurture yourself so that you can be healthy and happy. It does not mean giving in to pleasures or rewards that may compromise your physical and mental health and wellbeing. Taking care of your health and wellbeing often requires some effort and it can be difficult to motivate yourself to exercise, eat well and take care of yourself the same way you would take care of your child.

Self-punishment

Often when we notice something we don't like about ourselves and we want to try and change it we have this weird concept that if we shame ourselves into action we will be able to change it. Instead of being kind, understanding, encouraging and motivating ourselves to change we are critical, judgemental, discouraging and unmotivating. Self-compassion allows us to show the same understanding and encouragement we offer to others to ourselves.

Self-esteem

I believe it is important to discuss the difference between self-esteem and self-compassion. There has been a constant need for people to achieve a high level of self-esteem in order to be successful and accepted in our society. There is no doubt that low self-esteem can be problematic and can lead to isolation and depression, but there is also a lot of evidence to indicate that high self-esteem is also problematic. High self-esteem encourages us to be better than others, to stand out at any cost, to be special and to be the best.Although some of that sounds like a healthy view of ourselves, it often leads to people being who they are not. It invokes feelings of never being *"good enough"* and creates unnecessary comparisons and expectations to live up to. Our self-esteem is also directly dependent on what others think of us and our perceived successes and failures.

Self-compassion is based on how we accept and value ourselves. In order to feel good about who we are we do not need to be better than others or meet anyone else's expectations or be like anyone else. We just accept ourselves for who we are (warts and all!). This alleviates the feelings of not being *"good enough"* and the desire to prove to others who we are. Self-compassion fosters healthy self-esteem and that is what we should all be aiming for: a genuine acceptance of who we are and a healthy level of self-esteem.

What stops us from being self-compassionate?

There are several reasons why we resist the concept of self-compassion, not only because we think we need to put others before ourselves but also because of many fears we create in our minds. These fears include: the fear of self-pity and the danger of wallowing in our own suffering, the fear of facing and accepting our difficult emotions, the fear of failure, the fear of being judged by others, the fear of being self-indulgent, the fear of facing our own pain and suffering and the fear of accepting our own vulnerabilities.

There is also a fear of compassion itself, as many of us struggle to access our soothing and safety system that underpins compassion. This can be for many reasons but often it is the result of feeling unsafe as a child and not having our needs met in a nurturing, attentive way.

The first experiences of warmth, understanding and kindness we show to ourselves when we begin to be self-compassionate can cause difficult emotions such as sadness and grief to arise. This in turn may ignite feelings of shame for highly self-critical people. For some, these initial feelings may become overwhelming and they may give up rather than face the fears and accept the emotions. But with encouragement in a safe, supportive environment these fears can be addressed. The new-found skills of self-compassion create an opportunity for a new way of being and the ability to fully engage and immerse yourself in the life you are living.

Why is self-compassion important in motherhood?

After the findings in my research and working with many mothers throughout their motherhood experience, I have discovered that there is a lack of self-compassion in mothers regardless of whether they are first-time mums or third-time mums. This is probably no surprise! We know that becoming a mother is laden with responsibilities and expectations for yourself, your baby and others. Even mothers who have had wonderful self-care strategies before they have children find it difficult to maintain a sense of self-compassion throughout motherhood. If the concept of self-compassion becomes a focus in the motherhood experience it allows mothers to stop being so hard on themselves. To accept and deal with difficult emotions with more ease. To motivate themselves with encouragement rather than criticism. To attune more mindfully to their babies and to have a more meaningful experience. Join me in the following chapters to discover some insights on how to become a self-compassionate mother!

Chapter 5

Shadow Self

"To be yourself in a world that is constantly trying to make you someone else is the greatest accomplishment."
– Ralph Waldo Emmerson

As a result of my research and from my insights working with mothers, I have noticed *three* common themes weaving their way into the motherhood experience. These common themes create a stage for challenges and distress to play out and often *"cast shadows"* over the joy of motherhood.

The first one I would like to explore with you in this chapter is the theme of the *shadow self*, which is underpinned by *"unhelpful views of self"*. These unhelpful views we create of ourselves as mothers lead to that common feeling of not being *"good enough"*. This causes us to strive to be perfect mothers! But, as Jill Churchill says, *"There is no way to be a perfect mother but there are a million ways to be a good one!"* Striving for the elusive goal of being a perfect mother will only reinforce those negative views of yourself as not being *"good enough"*.

Where do unhelpful views come from?

Whether we like it or not we all have an *"inner critic"* – that voice in your head that is constantly judging and criticising you and causing you to feel not good enough in so many ways. Our inner critic develops as a result of our early negative experiences and messages we receive from others throughout our lives.

As humans we are designed to look out for danger as one of our most basic survival instincts. Although this is a great asset in many ways this high alert system that looks out for danger is also tuned into all the negative messages around us. This causes us to check them out to see if they are dangerous and we end up paying a lot of attention to them if they are painful or can hurt us in any way. The more of these negative messages we receive and take notice of, the stronger our inner critic becomes. The more evidence the inner critic has that you are a bad person, or you are *"not good enough"* the more it berates you and stops you from believing in yourself.

How many unhelpful labels have you identified with in the past from messages you have received? These may have been negative messages from family, school, partners, your workplace or friends. These unhelpful labels all contribute to us creating a negative view of ourselves and have a direct impact on our level of self-esteem, self-acceptance and self-worth.

When we are faced with transitions and challenges in life the inner critic has a field day and there is no greater transition or challenge for a woman than becoming a mother. So, it makes sense that this inner critic becomes incredibly active from the moment you conceive or decide to embark on the journey of becoming a mother. Although we all have this inner critic it is how we react and respond to it that makes the difference as to how much influence it has on our experiences in life.

My research identified six underlying factors that contributed significantly to mothers' unhelpful views of themselves: judgement from others, self-judgement, lack of productivity, lack of self-care, lack of self-worth, and social comparisons.

Judgement from others
We all feel judged by others at some point in our lives and this feeling is very dominant in motherhood. It is responsible for the high levels of self-doubt that mothers report feeling. One of the most common forms of feeling judged as a mother relates to the concept constantly imposed on mothers: *"Enjoy it while it lasts – life won't get any better than it is now"*. Although this statement from others may be well-meaning and intended to encourage mothers to embrace the experience, it more often than not creates a sense of embarrassment and guilt. Mothers who are not necessarily enjoying every moment are fearful of saying anything in case they are judged.

Another common form of judgement from others comes from the way mothers choose to re-engage in the workforce and leave their babies with family members or in day care. As one of the mothers I was working with stated: *"I had to go away for work when my baby was only eight months old – my sister, mother and most of my friends who had children kept asking me how I could do it. I constantly felt like people were judging me for making the decision to go and it made it very difficult – I really felt like I was not being a 'good enough' mother in their eyes"*.

Mothers are judged from the moment they become pregnant and throughout their child's life. They are judged by others for how they handle their pregnancy, what they do and don't eat or drink, if they do too much or too little exercise, if they choose to have a natural home birth or a caesarean section, if they do not breastfeed or if they breastfeed for too long. Mothers are questioned for not following the controlled crying method to get their babies to sleep or for following it. They are judged for going back to work too soon or for not going back to work and so the list goes on and on. There is very little a mother can do without being judged by someone. It takes a lot of commitment, courage and confidence to overcome the judgements and not allow them to infiltrate and influence how we see ourselves as mothers.

Judgement of Self

It goes without saying that the judgement from others triggers in each of us an element of self-doubt and self-criticism. Our inner critic loves evidence from others that we are not good enough and it uses this evidence to create a whole story around doubting our own capabilities and skills. For mothers, this self-doubt creates a fear and vulnerability that we are perceived as a not *"good enough mother"*. This element of self-doubt and self-criticism causes us to second guess everything we do. This is not only exhausting but it takes us away from following our instinct and noticing what is important for our baby and ourselves. Instead of focusing on getting our needs and our baby's needs met we become fused with unhelpful thoughts of what we should be doing and what others are doing better than us. We forget to notice what we are doing well and affirming ourselves that we are *"good enough"*. I have yet to come across a mother who is not hard on herself and who is not constantly second-guessing herself and looking for reassurance from others that she is doing a good job; even mothers who are having their second or third child report experiencing high levels of self-doubt and self-criticism.

Lack of Self-worth

Once we take on the judgement from others and our own self-judgement there is only one guaranteed outcome: our level of self-worth and self-acceptance will plummet to an all-time low. Some of us are more prone to low levels of self-esteem and self-worth as a result of our early life experiences. Moving back into this way of viewing ourselves in the world comes naturally and it is even more difficult to recognise that it has happened. If our levels of self-worth and self-acceptance are low, we step into living a life that is not aligned with who we truly are, a life certainly not aligned with our core values. Mothers who step into this way of being are in constant conflict with trying to be like others and trying to be themselves. They are always living in the shadow of others and trying to meet other's expectations. In doing this they lose sight of not only themselves but also their babies. Their experience of motherhood is scripted by others and all the joy and personal meaning is taken out of the experience.

Lack of Productivity

In today's fast-paced society most women have very productive lives prior to becoming mothers. It is a common theme in counselling that they report being under-prepared for the lack of productivity they would achieve on a day-to-day basis. On exploring this more with mothers, I have discovered that most of them do not consider the tasks of motherhood to be productive and they are constantly judging themselves for not achieving enough. Productivity and achievement in today's world seems to revolve around instant, measurable results that are affirmed by everyone around us. This is an incredibly unrealistic goal in motherhood as the tasks are often repetitive, not measurable, unpredictable and often go unnoticed and unappreciated by most people around us. They are just expected tasks of motherhood that we are supposed to achieve without recognition.

Lack of Self-Care

At a time when we need to be more focused than ever on our self-care, it surprises me how many mothers say to me, *"I just don't have time to take care of myself"*. Motherhood seems to be a time when women cannot give themselves permission to put their self-care as a priority. It seems as though the thought of taking care of themselves invokes feelings of being self-indulgent and not being able to justify giving back to themselves. The focus and attention all seems to be on their baby, their partner, their family and their friends. This need to care for everyone else exhausts them and actually makes them less available to care for others. I am constantly amazed by women who for most of their lives have recognised the importance of self-care and the need to give back to themselves, yet when they become mothers that all goes out the window! They are on the bottom of the list to be cared for. Are you guilty of this? Have you stopped taking care of yourself and doing the things that make you feel good? Most of us know what helps relieve our levels of stress, what makes us feel relaxed and find the joy in life. So why do we stop doing something that is working? I know that the early days and weeks of becoming a mother can be exhausting and at times it does seem like there are not enough hours in the day. You will be surprised at how much more time you will have if you bring back some simple self-care strategies into your daily routine.

Social Comparisons

Whether we like it or not part of the shared human experience is that we compare ourselves to others. Motherhood is no exception to this concept and it is natural for mothers to compare themselves to their own mothers, sisters, and friends who in their eyes have managed the tasks and responsibilities of motherhood so well and who they aspire to be like. But instead of these comparisons resulting in a motivation to be the best possible version of a mother you can be, these comparisons more often than not result in feelings of failure and self-doubt.

The concept of mother's groups has been around for decades and it was introduced to help mothers connect with each other and offer support and a sense of community. On the whole, mother's groups have been a helpful source of connection and a place where mothers could openly talk about their fears, worries and joys of being a mother. But as our culture and society has become more materialistic and individualistic there seems to have been a shift in the intention of mother's groups. I have seen several mothers who have not had a very positive experience in mother's groups. They have felt more isolated and alone than they were before they joined. They have reported feeling judged by the other mothers and have found themselves constantly comparing their baby's development with other babies in the group. As we all know, we are not going to naturally feel connected to a group of strangers. However, I do believe that if we can find the ability to accept each mother and child as unique, we would be more open and curious and more accepting of our differences.

The digital age has brought with it an invaluable source of information and connection, but it has also brought with it a platform for social comparisons and disconnection. Social media sites, blogs, the Internet, and support groups have been reported by mothers as being unhelpful. They increase the pressure to be the *"perfect mother who can do it all with a smile on her face and a social profile of suburban bliss"*. I do believe there are some forms of social media and groups that have been incredibly helpful for mothers who are feeling isolated and alone, but choose wisely. Make a conscious decision as to why it is that you are choosing to join or follow any social media profiles or groups. Below are some of the issues mothers have spoken about that have not been helpful in social media.

Looking for support and advice: *"Sometimes it was just useful to know that other people were going through the same kind of thing ... but then there were other things where you were trying to look for advice and that can be difficult ... because then you can get very conflicting advice ... "*

Comparing yourself to the unrealistic portrayal of motherhood on social media: *"Comparing yourself to these dream kids that other people have is just not helpful ... "*

"Always comparing your baby and yourself to people that are very different to you ... "

Trying to find the right way to breastfeed: *"I look on the Internet far too much and diagnose things that I don't need to be diagnosing, especially around breastfeeding."*

There are many more ways that mothers create unhelpful views of themselves and I am sure most of you would be able to create a long list of how you view yourself as *"not good enough"* and how many negative labels you have identified with in the past. I would encourage you to spend some time reflecting on your inner critic, noticing how often you are tuning into the negative messages and judgements on a day-to-day basis.

Here is an exercise that you may find useful that I give to my clients. Try and tune into your inner critic and notice the tone of voice it uses – is it loud or soft? Does it remind you of anyone? Do you see any colours when you tune into your inner critic? Do you notice any images – what does your inner critic look like? On a piece of paper jot down some of the things you have identified in your inner critic, if you are feeling creative try and draw your inner critic. Some of you may be thinking why would we want to identify it and take notice of it if we are trying to quieten it down? You will be amazed that once you have identified the inner critic and perhaps even given it a name it will be much easier for you to notice the critic and to be able to invite it to quieten down and eventually become less active. Some of my clients have made or bought something that represents their inner critic and they keep it somewhere to remind them that the inner critic is only a part of us. It does not need to consume us. We have a choice as to how we react and respond to the voice of the inner critic. Good luck identifying your inner critic and may he or she become a quiet voice in the background of your life instead of a loud voice in the foreground of your life.

Chapter 6

True Self

"A second quality of mature spirituality is kindness. It is based on the fundamental notion of self-acceptance."
– Jack Kornfield

In my experience working as a counsellor and as a result of the findings in my research, the *three shadows* of motherhood can be overcome by the *three* elements of self-compassion. The first shadow of motherhood, *shadow self*, which is a result of unhelpful views we have of ourselves can be overcome by the first element of self-compassion, which has been defined as *self-kindness*.

Self-kindness is described as the ability to show kindness to ourselves instead of giving in to the inner critic with self-doubt and judgement. In my work with clients, especially mothers, I am astounded by how difficult the concept of self-kindness is for people to put into practice.

We are born to be kind and take care of our authentic selves, but we quickly lose the ability in order to fit in and meet the expectations of others. If you can't be kind, accepting and understanding towards yourself, then it is very difficult to show true kindness and acceptance to others.

Self-kindness allows for warmth and understanding: it alleviates feelings of inadequacy and failure. Self-kindness encourages us to tap into our natural caregiving system and soothe ourselves in times of emotional, physical or psychological suffering. Just the same as we feel safe and secure when someone nurtures us and shows us kindness and understanding, so showing ourselves kindness and understanding generates an internal sense of safety. Self-kindness is also an essential source of self-acceptance and allows us to be who we truly are – our *true self*.

> "You can search throughout the entire universe for someone who is more deserving of your love and affection than you are yourself, and that person is not to be found anywhere. You, yourself, as much as anybody in the entire universe, deserve your love and affection."
> Buddha

Key strategies for self-kindness

The first strategy is to notice the language you use: is it the voice of the inner critic, or is it a kind caring voice that is accepting and encouraging? You will be surprised when you begin to notice the language you use with yourself on a day-to-day basis. I doubt it is the way you would speak to a good friend or someone you really cared about. Just changing your language, tone of voice and words you use on a daily basis will change the way you think and feel about yourself.

Remember: "You will never speak to anyone more than you do to yourself in your head so speak kindly to yourself".

If you really struggle with this concept it is sometimes easier to ask yourself in difficult times or times of suffering, "What would I say to a good friend?" then say those kind words to yourself and notice how it makes you feel. Notice your self-talk and the language you use with yourself on a daily basis, not only in difficult times but all the time.

Do you need to change it?

Have you given in to your inner critic?

Is it controlling the way you think and feel about yourself?

The second strategy for self-kindness is self-care – giving yourself permission to take care of yourself as you would take care of someone who you loved and appreciated. All too often our own self-care is the one thing that we seem to never be able to find time for until we are forced to because we are physically, emotionally or psychologically unwell.

There is no evidence to suggest that taking time out for self-care is unproductive, self-indulgent or selfish, yet it seems like the hardest task to achieve, especially in motherhood. As mothers we feel like we are on-call 24/7 for our children. The reality is that a little self-care everyday will make you a better mother – more emotionally, physically and psychologically available.

Self-care does not have to be hours spent at the gym or hours of meditation. It can be the simple things in life like making sure you take time to shower, have a cup of tea, eat healthy food, go for a short walk, listen to your favourite music, draw or paint, relax in your garden listening to the birds, or simply noticing what it feels like to be in nature, under a tree or at the beach watching the sights and sounds around you. We have, as a society, lost touch with the simple concept of self-care and the sooner you re-introduce it on a daily basis the sooner you will be able to grasp the concept of self-kindness. Let's face it: if you can't take care of yourself you can't possibly be trusted to take care of others – especially a baby.

Whilst you are going through the process of re-introducing self-care into your daily routine you might find it useful to keep a note of one self-care activity or strategy you have put into place on a daily basis. The only way we can learn new habits is by acknowledging them and reinforcing them. By allowing ourselves to recognise how good they make us feel, how different we feel about ourselves when we do them. Try and do this exercise daily for a month and notice how you think and feel about yourself.

The third strategy is to value, affirm and encourage yourself. Compassionate people have a natural ability to value, affirm and encourage others they care about. If you have not had much encouragement and have not felt valued by others, then it is very difficult to do this for yourself. I am always saddened by how little people value themselves in life, especially mothers – they often do not see the value in their role as mothers and they certainly are not very good at showing themselves any encouragement or affirmation.

They are, however, incredibly good at offering encouragement, validation and affirmation to other mothers. Again, this is a vital step in showing yourself true kindness, valuing your role and validating yourself as a mother or mother-to-be.

Notice the tasks you achieve every day, affirm yourself on a daily basis and reassure yourself that you are doing a great job. Think of how you have validated other mothers in the past and how you have supported and encouraged them to value and believe in themselves. Find the same kind words and say them to yourself. In order to practice this strategy of valuing, affirming and encouraging yourself, try and record three things you feel you did well or appreciate about yourself on a daily basis. Again, try this for a month and see if your levels of self-kindness have increased and notice how you feel and think about yourself.

Self-acceptance

The practice of self-kindness cannot be fully achieved if we do not master the art of self-acceptance – the ability to accept our true authentic self. So, the million-dollar question is who is the true authentic self? I like to think that our true authentic self is the unique, one-of-a-kind blueprint that is made up of our personality, our strengths and weaknesses, our core values, our life experiences and our passions.

Personality

The word personality stems from the Latin word "persona", which was used to refer to a mask worn by actors to portray different roles or disguise their identity. Our personality is made up of traits, thoughts, feelings and behaviours unique to each individual. Both genetic and environmental factors contribute to the development of our personality. There are many theories of personality and nowadays there are a large number of ways to test our personality type.

The most important thing is for you to embrace your unique personality and accept all the traits that come with it. There are far too many of us out there living behind the mask of who we truly are and constantly wasting time and energy trying to be who we are not. Are you wearing a mask? Whose mask are you wearing? What would it be like to step out of the shadow of your mask and into your true self? Embrace your personality and your true identity.

Positive Qualities

Most clients I have worked with can give me a list of their weaknesses or negative qualities very easily. In fact, they often fill up the whole whiteboard. Very few can give me a list of their positive qualities or strengths. It is almost secret squirrel business to discuss our positive qualities openly for fear of being judged for boasting or *"blowing our own trumpet"*.

In order to truly accept ourselves we need to have a balanced evaluation of ourselves, noticing both our positive and negative qualities without focusing more on one or the other. People with low self-esteem or low self-worth seem to be over-identified with the negative qualities they possess. They lose sight of any positive qualities they may have. If you are having difficulty as you are reading this in being able to identify your positive qualities, perhaps you could start by creating a positive qualities record. Ask yourself some of these simple questions:

What do I like about who I am?

What positive characteristics do I have?

What are some of my achievements in life?

What challenges have I overcome in the past?

What skills or talents do I possess?

What do others say about me?

How might someone who cares about me describe me? (If you don't know ask a good friend, your partner or a close family member to describe you.)

As you do this exercise try and notice if that inner critic jumps in and minimises anything positive you have to say about yourself. See if you can quieten it down and focus your attention on the recognition of these qualities. Once you have identified some positive qualities you may like to print out a list of positive qualities from the Internet and circle the qualities you identify with. Notice how you feel about yourself when you truly accept and identify the positive qualities of your true authentic self.

Values

We all have a set of unique core values that define who we are, what we stand for and how we want to behave in the world around us. According to Russ Harris, the well-known author of *The Happiness Trap*, values are *"your heart's deepest desires"* (Russ Harris, 2007). There are so many lists of values out there, but the list below has been compiled by Russ Harris (2010). It is commonly used in therapy and provides a comprehensive list of the most common values. You may not relate to all the values listed but keep in mind that there are no right or wrong values or good or bad values. As I have said many times in this book so far, we are all unique and we all come with a unique set of values, so keep an open mind and try and identify the values that you relate more to.

As you go through the list below, write a letter next to each value – V = Very important, Q = Quite important, and N = Not so important – and try not to score more than six of them as very important.

- Acceptance: to be open to and accepting of myself, others, life
- Adventure: to be adventurous; to actively seek, create, or explore novel or stimulating experiences
- Assertiveness: to respectfully stand up for my rights and request what I want
- Authenticity: to be authentic, genuine, real; to be true to myself

- Beauty: to appreciate, create, nurture or cultivate beauty in myself, others, the environment
- Caring: to be caring towards myself, others, the environment
- Challenge: to keep challenging myself to grow, learn, improve
- Compassion: to act with kindness towards those who are suffering
- Connection: to engage fully in whatever I am doing, and be fully present with others
- Contribution: to contribute, help, assist, or make a positive difference to myself or others
- Conformity: to be respectful and obedient of rules and obligations
- Cooperation: to be cooperative and collaborative with others
- Courage: to be courageous or brave; to persist in the face of fear, threat, or difficulty
- Creativity: to be creative or innovative
- Curiosity: to be curious, open-minded and interested; to explore and discover
- Encouragement: to encourage and reward behaviour that I value in myself or others
- Equality: to treat others as equal to myself, and vice-versa
- Excitement: to seek, create and engage in activities that are exciting, stimulating or thrilling
- Fairness: to be fair to myself or others
- Fitness: to maintain or improve my fitness; to look after my physical and mental health and wellbeing
- Flexibility: to adjust and adapt readily to changing circumstances
- Freedom: to live freely; to choose how I live and behave, or help others do likewise
- Friendliness: to be friendly, companionable, or agreeable towards others
- Forgiveness: to be forgiving towards myself or others
- Fun: to be fun-loving; to seek, create, and engage in fun-filled activities
- Generosity: to be generous, sharing and giving, to myself or others

- Gratitude: to be grateful for and appreciative of the positive aspects of myself, others and life
- Honesty: to be honest, truthful, and sincere with myself and others
- Humour: to see and appreciate the humorous side of life
- Humility: to be humble or modest; to let my achievements speak for themselves
- Industry: to be industrious, hard-working, dedicated
- Independence: to be self-supportive, and choose my own way of doing things
- Intimacy: to open up, reveal, and share myself -- emotionally or physically – in my close personal relationships
- Justice: to uphold justice and fairness
- Kindness: to be kind, compassionate, considerate, nurturing or caring towards myself or others
- Love: to act lovingly or affectionately towards myself or others
- Mindfulness: to be conscious of, open to, and curious about my here-and-now experience
- Order: to be orderly and organized
- Open-mindedness: to think things through, see things from other's points of view, and weigh evidence fairly.
- Patience: to wait calmly for what I want
- Persistence: to continue resolutely, despite problems or difficulties.
- Pleasure: to create and give pleasure to myself or others
- Power: to strongly influence or wield authority over others, e.g. taking charge, leading, organizing
- Reciprocity: to build relationships in which there is a fair balance of giving and taking
- Respect: to be respectful towards myself or others; to be polite, considerate and show positive regard
- Responsibility: to be responsible and accountable for my actions
- Romance: to be romantic; to display and express love or strong affection
- Safety: to secure, protect, or ensure safety of myself or others

- Self-awareness: to be aware of my own thoughts, feelings and actions
- Self-care: to look after my health and wellbeing, and get my needs met
- Self-development: to keep growing, advancing or improving in knowledge, skills, character, or life experience.
- Self-control: to act in accordance with my own ideals
- Sensuality: to create, explore and enjoy experiences that stimulate the five senses
- Sexuality: to explore or express my sexuality
- Spirituality: to connect with things bigger than myself
- Skilfulness: to continually practice and improve my skills, and apply myself fully when using them
- Supportiveness: to be supportive, helpful, encouraging, and available to myself or others
- Trust: to be trustworthy; to be loyal, faithful, sincere, and reliable.

Write your six top values on a piece of paper, on a post-it note or on your mobile phone. Keep it anywhere that you can see it on a daily basis. Try and notice if you are living your life and making decisions in accordance with your values, or if are you compromising your values to fit in or please others. Are you trying to be someone else?

Life experiences

Our life experiences, culture and environment have a direct impact on our personality. It is believed that our life experiences influence and shape how we see the world around us, how we structure our core beliefs, how we relate to others and our ability to cope in the face of challenges and life difficulties. Our personality and culture influence our ability to cope. The younger we are when we are exposed to difficult or traumatic experiences, the less ability we have to cope. There are some experiences in life we wish had never happened and we wish we had dealt with them differently.

None of us are exempt from these feelings of resentment and remorse. It is, however, important for us to understand how our past life experiences have influenced us and what assumptions, beliefs and stories we have created around the experiences that may not be serving us well now. It is not common practice for us to question our beliefs and assumptions with an open, curious mind, or for us to try and discover if there is a way to change these core beliefs and assumptions that may be standing in our way of connecting with others or living a meaningful life.

> "Experience is not what happens to a man. It is what a man does with what happens to him."
> – Aldous Leonard Huxley

When we take the time to notice how our past experiences have influenced us and how our choice of reaction to these experiences has influenced our personality, we allow ourselves the opportunity to choose to react differently. We can choose to rewrite the scripts we have written about the world around us.

This realisation also gives us the opportunity to choose to create positive experiences for others around us and make them feel safe and connected. Understanding the influence of negative and positive past experiences in your life and the way they have shaped who you are provides you with an opportunity to ensure your child is given the best opportunity to have positive experiences in life.

Passion

There is no meaning in life if we do not follow our heart and align ourselves with things we are passionate about. We are all born with a unique set of passions, inspirations and interests that guide us to connect with our true purpose and make our life meaningful. As children we imagine great things we will achieve and believe we can conquer the world. We try anything and do anything. As we grow into adulthood and are confined by the rules, assumptions and expectations of society we lose touch with this source of purpose. Our dreams, desires, interests and passions get placed on hold and hidden away, sometimes never to be found. The level of dissatisfaction and discontentment in our society today is evidence of how many of us have locked away the seeds of inspiration that make life meaningful to us.

So, what is your passion? It is that thing that lights you up from the inside out, it is that thing that we talk or dream about often, it is that thing that we find ourselves talking about with people who are genuinely interested in us. What we are passionate about connects us to our soul and makes our heart beat faster and our energy levels rise. What are your passions, dreams, desires or interests that you have given up on? They form an integral part of who you truly are. They allow you to connect with your true authentic self. Be brave, step out of your status quo comfort zone and embrace one of your passions in life. It will make the process of accepting yourself for who you truly are more enjoyable!

*

As you can see, in order to begin the practice of self-kindness you first have to find, connect and accept your true authentic self. Get to know who you truly are and what you stand for in life – understand where your values and beliefs have come from and choose how you want to live your life. Let's face it, we all find it difficult to be kind to someone who we do not like, accept or connect with, so how can you truly be kind to yourself if you do not find out what it is that you like, love, appreciate and accept about your true self? May you find the courage to step out from behind your mask and be who you were born to be!

Chapter 7

Shadow Expectations

"If you have too much expectation you may come away disappointed."
– Dalai Lama

The *second shadow* that is common for many mothers is that of *"unmet expectations"*: the expectations mothers have of themselves as well as what they think others expect from them. These expectations cause unnecessary distress and are often the major causes of depression and anxiety in the perinatal period. The gap between reality and unmet expectations is filled with anxiety and causes us to lose sight of reality in the pursuit of unrealistic expectations.

What are expectations?

One of our greatest challenges in life is mastering the art of realistic expectations. Expectations are not our future reality but rather beliefs we have accepted about the future. These expectations are often based on our previous life experiences, messages we have received from others around us and the human need to feel accepted and connected. We need expectations to drive us to pursue our dreams and to better ourselves and as a source of motivation. But our expectations of ourselves and others are often unrealistic. We set ourselves and others up to fail because of these unrealistic expectations.

Have you ever thought about where your expectations have come from and whose expectations you are trying to live up to? You will find that you can trace some of your unrealistic expectations back to a time when you were trying to get your parents, siblings, school teachers or friends attention or approval and failed. For some reason not meeting others' expectations makes us put pressure on ourselves and creates even more unrealistic expectations. Deep down inside we know we cannot live up to, but we will continue to create, these unrealistic and unachievable expectations.

Those of you who are perfectionists will be all too familiar with setting yourself unrealistic expectations, never achieving them or even attempting them as the fear of failure leaves you frozen and finding all the excuses under the sun as to why you can't achieve these expectations. As a result, what we see is that all too familiar concept of perfectionists being procrastinators.

As I mentioned earlier, the gap between realistic and unrealistic expectations, not only for mothers but also for everyone in our society, is filled with unnecessary anxiety. Realistic and consciously chosen expectations can motivate us to achieve and accept our reality.

My research delved into some of the unrealistic expectations mothers experience and identified *four* key areas of unmet expectations. They were unmet expectations of the motherhood experience, unmet expectations of others, unmet expectations of themselves and unmet expectations of support. The gap between reality and expectations for some mothers becomes a source of emotional and psychological distress that they find difficult to manage and may result in elevated levels of anxiety and or depression.

Expectations of motherhood experience

Whether we like it or not we will have expectations around our overall experience of becoming a mother. These expectations may be based on the experiences of our own mother, sisters or friends, or be based on societal views and stereotypical constructs. Mothers are more often than not very unprepared for the transition from their identity before their babies come along to their identity as a mother and this was very evident in my research.

There is an expectation that this will happen naturally and that there is no preparation needed and that life will still be productive and you will still be able to *"do it all"*. If you recall from Chapter 1, this is often not the case and not the reality. As one mother in my research implied, being a mother is unlike a regular job; mothers are unable to resign if the tasks are not enjoyable. She said, *"I suppose you invest so much in it and if you were in a job you were not enjoying you know ... in the real professional world you wouldn't stay there."*

The overall expected experience of motherhood is not all it's made out to be for many of the mothers I have worked with. They feel it is like being *"thrown in the deep end"* as there are many challenges that they encountered that they were not prepared for. In my research, mothers report their overall experience as being a *"wild ride full of unexpected challenges"* and they all agreed that you cannot explain what it is like to be around a new born and be in demand 24/7 until you have your own. Some of the mothers also reported not being prepared for the physical stress on their bodies during pregnancy and after birth. However, most mothers would not take back the experience and they admit there were times of joy in amongst the challenges. They were all in agreement that there needs to be more openness in discussing the reality of the motherhood experience so women can be more prepared for the transition.

Expectations of others

We all want to be perceived as *"good enough"* in all we do in life and becoming a mother is no exception to this quest in life. There is a common myth that if we meet others' expectations of us then we will be accepted, loved and appreciated by them. The problem is that often these expectations are unrealistic and unachievable. The pressure we put on ourselves as mothers to live up to the expectations of others creates unnecessary stress and discomfort in an already challenging time.

One of the most common expectations from others is that you will *"enjoy this time, as it is one of the most enjoyable times in a woman's life"*. The reality is aspects of motherhood are incredibly enjoyable but there are difficult times that most certainly cannot be described as enjoyable. When mothers put on a brave face and pretend to the world around them that everything is going just fine they are often masking the reality of their own struggles and suffering. The fact that they are not really enjoying everything about motherhood creates feelings of guilt and shame. They often end up denying any signs of anxiety and depression until they can no longer cope.

Other people's expectations can at times make mothers feel like they are being criticised for doing things their way instead of trying to fit in and do things the way others have done. As one mother stated: *"Every choice I made I was criticised and someone (mostly my family) had something to say about it and I ended up listening to everyone else and struggling to figure out what I should do, which expectations I should listen to."*

The expectations of others are all around you as a mother and it is important to focus on your reality and choose which and whose expectations you are trying to live up to. Notice if this is making your experience of motherhood more enjoyable or creating a lot of unnecessary stress and pressure.

Expectations of Self

Most mothers have high expectations of themselves in their role as a mother and they put a lot of unrealistic pressure on themselves to do everything "right". There is a tendency when we are trying to meet our own expectations to focus on what we are not doing well or achieving rather than what we are doing well or achieving. This way of thinking creates a self-fulfilling prophecy that we are never going to be able to live up to our own expectations. This causes us to lose focus on the present and live in the unrealistic future where we supposedly will be able to live up to all our expectations. One mother said, *"That was a big thing for me, you know, when you have these expectations of yourself and what you are going to achieve and you know that you are not going to get anything done."*

Whether you are a first-time mother or a second- or third-time mother you will have expectations of yourself. What I have found interesting is that second- and third-time mothers often have more expectations of themselves than the first time around. There is an assumption that if you have had one child you know how to do it and everything will be so much easier. You will do things differently as you learnt from the first. Whilst this assumption may be true for some mothers, it is not the case for all mothers. As one of the mothers stated, *"I hadn't prepared myself for the expectation that he could be as difficult as my first one, then when he was I thought I just can't do it again, I just can't repeat that again ... I had this whole idea of what it was going to be like and it just got crushed when reality set in"*.

Probably one of the most common expectations I have seen many mothers set for themselves is this one: *"I must have a natural birth and I will only breastfeed my baby"*. As a result of this, I have witnessed the distress, heartache and pain that have resulted when this seemingly simple, achievable expectation is not met. There are many stories like this and the angst and pain caused by unmet birthing, bonding and breastfeeding expectations is one of the root causes of depression and anxiety in motherhood.

Expectations of support

Although we live in an individualistic society there is the hope that, at significant times in our lives, we will have the support of loved ones and professionals. Motherhood is one of those times when it is acceptable to reach out and seek this kind of support. We have an expectation that we will get the support we need.

The reality is that this support is not always so easily accessible and often comes with its own set of conditions and expectations.

Mothers often report to me that they feared seeking support from professionals such as doctors, counsellors, child health nurses and other health professionals. They believed they might have been judged and may be at risk of having their babies taken away. Even when they were experiencing emotional suffering and were not coping they admitted to "lying" on the EPDS (Edinburgh Post-Natal Depression Scale) and DASS (Depression, Anxiety and Stress Scale) assessments as they were fearful of the outcome.

Mothers reported to me that they would prefer someone to sit them down and talk to them about what was really going on for them on a day-to-day basis, instead of giving them a form to fill out and then offering them ten minutes of their time and rushing them out the door! Just as one mother reported, *"I didn't seek help, I know I could have asked for help but I find the questionnaires quite extreme – you know, the EPDS and the DASS – I find it very easy to lie in them. You can just say, 'I don't feel anxious at all'. So I think if someone had truly sat down and talked to me I think I would have burst into tears and a lot of things would have come out, instead of this ten minute appointment that you have and you just fill it out and hand it into the receptionist and just go."*

New mothers report that they are often dismissed by health professionals when they do try and seek support. This results in them feeling discouraged, doubting themselves and not seeking support when they need it the most, believing they should be able to cope on their own.

One desperate mother came to see me after she had tried to get professional help, as she could not sleep at night when she was pregnant. She was working at the time and was exhausted. She had sought help through her doctor and had been told that it was quite common for women to struggle with sleep during pregnancy and there was not much she could offer as a solution but that *"women who do not sleep during pregnancy are more prone to developing post-natal depression"*. By the time I saw her, she was beside herself with worry about the possibility of post-natal depression and, as you can imagine, her sleep was worse than ever. She was exhausted.

There is a system in place to support mothers and there is an expectation that it will be there to support them but there are times when this does not happen. The most important thing to remember as a mother is that there is helpful support out there. Do not give up and do not think that you are supposed to cope on your own. Reach out until you find the professional support you are looking for.

Partners, family, friends and other mums are often a source of invaluable support for mothers, but if our expectations are too unrealistic in this regard it can be a source of disappointment and frustration. Well-meaning family members and partners often try and offer support in the form of advice. This can be misinterpreted by mothers as judgement or criticism. As one mother stated, *"They don't actually do much apart from give their two bits of advice"*. Although support is often readily available from loved ones and friends, mothers find it difficult to ask for what they need in case it is perceived as them not coping or not being *"good enough"*. Partners or significant others regularly report to me that they want to offer help and support but they don't know what to do or how to help. They normally end up doing nothing or doing something that is not appreciated. Partners, family and friends are not *"mind readers"* and sometimes mothers are their own worst enemies. They do not give themselves permission to ask for what they need. If you have expectations of your partner, family or friends, allow them to know what they might be. Allow them to at least attempt to meet your needs and expectations.

Realistic Expectations

If it were possible I would ask you to have no expectations in your motherhood experience! But that would be almost impossible as we are only human and we all have expectations. Be aware of the expectations you are setting for yourself and others in your motherhood experience. Be curious as to where and why these expectations have come about and reality check them. Are they achievable? Do you have the internal and external resources to meet the expectations you are setting for yourself? Are others around you capable of meeting your expectations or have you set them up to fail? Remember every child is unique, every mother is unique! No two motherhood experiences are the same. Don't have too many expectations and let go of the need to meet other's expectations. The journey will be far more enjoyable. You and your baby will not be under constant pressure to conform to expectations.

Chapter 8

True Expectations

"If you align your expectations with reality you will never be disappointed."
– Terrell Owens

The *second way* to overcome the shadows of motherhood is accepting that we are all human and learning to be human. One of the elements of self-compassion is *common humanity*. Common humanity is the recognition that as humans we are imperfect and that we are not alone in our suffering. We cannot always get what we want or expect. We cannot always be who we want to be. We are not alone in our imperfection as this is a fact of life shared by all humans. It is our imperfection that allows us to be part of the human race. Despite this common understanding, we often feel isolated and alone in our struggles and failures and end up with the irrational thoughts and feelings of, *"This is only happening to me"* or, *"It's only me who is having such a hard time"*. We begin to believe that we are not normal and that we are *"not good enough"*. We lose sight of the fact that failure and imperfection are actually a "normal" part of being human, experiences shared by all of us. Common humanity refers to the acceptance and understanding of the shared human experience, including the acceptance of suffering in the face of failure and the ability to deal with unmet expectations with compassion and understanding.

Dealing with unmet expectations

Regardless of how realistic we set our expectations, we are only human. We will always feel a sense of failure when we do not meet our own or others' expectations. The first part of dealing with unmet expectations is the acceptance of them: the recognition that we are all human and we all fail, but that does not mean that we are not good enough or that we need to beat ourselves up over our failures. When we perceive we have failed and not met our own or other's expectations we tend to isolate ourselves instead of reaching out and connecting. Being isolated and alone is one of the major causes of depression and anxiety, but feeling connected and cared for provides comfort from the pain of failure.

The fact is all mothers at some point feel like they are the only ones experiencing challenges and they feel guilty for not enjoying being a mother. The common humanity element of self-compassion helps us to accept and acknowledge our failures and suffering, share the experience, normalise the feelings and makes us feel connected to others. Let me share a few examples of how the common humanity element of self-compassion can help overcome the shadow cast by unmet expectations in motherhood.

Expectations of Motherhood Experience

Monique came to see me when she was four months pregnant. She had been living in Perth for three years and all her family were in Europe. She had a loving, supportive partner and she loved her job. The baby was planned. She had been looking forward to being pregnant. She came to me to help her as she had noticed she was feeling very depressed and just wasn't herself.

Monique had always wanted to be a mum, she had dreamed of being pregnant and had an expectation that it was going to be a beautiful experience and she was going to be radiant and glowing – just like her sister when she had her babies (*this is a common shared expectation for many new mothers*).

Monique suffered from morning sickness in the early months and felt awful: she had quite a few days off work and was still not feeling great and she was tired and tearful a lot of the time. Monique was very distressed as she told me she often wished she wasn't pregnant and did not feel any connection to the baby – this caused her to feel so ashamed and guilty and she could not share her thoughts with anyone. The gap between her reality and her expectation of becoming a mum was filled with uncomfortable emotions that not only resulted in her feeling anxious, but also in her becoming depressed.

Monique believed that every woman who is pregnant feels an automatic connection to their unborn child and this expectation that she could not meet made her feel like a failure. It made her think she did not deserve to have a baby.

We worked together to allow her to let go of the expectations she was trying to live up to – not only hers, but what she thought others expected of her. As the months went by and she felt physically stronger she developed a deep emotional connection to her unborn son. I asked her what she would say to other mothers and this is what she said: "*Free yourself from any preconceived expectations you may have about yourself or your baby – they rob you of your true connection and experience. Give over to the experience and ride the waves – they always come gently back to the shore.*"

Expectations of Self

"I must have a natural birth and I will only breastfeed my baby." This is a common expectation I have seen many mothers set for themselves and I have witnessed the distress, heartache and pain that has resulted when this seemingly simple, achievable expectation is not met. I will share with you Alice's story.

Alice was a beautiful soul who lived a healthy, wholesome life and was a practicing natural medicine practitioner. Alice attended a group I was running for mums-to-be. She shared her thoughts and views on birthing, breastfeeding and the expectations she had for her own motherhood experience. Although she was well aware that she had to be prepared for other birthing options, she still set a very clear expectation that the birth would be natural and at home. She had done everything she could to make sure she had a nutrient-rich supply of milk and that she would be able to breastfeed.

Unfortunately, Alice ended up having an emergency C-section under general anaesthetic and had a rough few days after the birth. Bonding and breastfeeding did not come as naturally as she had hoped.

By the time Alice came to see me for counselling, her baby girl was six weeks old and Alice was exhausted, depressed and anxious. The disappointment of not having a natural birth bundled with the guilt she felt for not being able to give birth naturally had taken a lot of the joy out of her experience so far. Breastfeeding was difficult for her and she was persevering, but her baby was taking an hour to feed.

Alice was not sleeping, was too exhausted to exercise and take care of herself. She had never experienced any anxiety or depression in the past and she felt like she was on an emotional rollercoaster. Reaching out for counselling was also difficult, as she had not had to ask for much help in her life.

For the next few months we worked together to give Alice some strategies to manage her emotional rollercoaster, set more realistic expectations for herself and her baby. We also found a way for her to make peace with the decision to bottle feed and breastfeed without considering herself a failure. We reduced the gap between her expectations and her reality and she was able to accept her human shared experience of not being perfect.

There are many more stories like this and the angst and pain caused by unmet birthing, bonding and breastfeeding expectations is one of the root causes of depression and anxiety in motherhood. If Alice had managed to have no expectations or more realistic expectations around birthing, breastfeeding and bonding, I believe her experience would have been a more joyful one. The reality is that a large number of women struggle to breastfeed; many mothers report not having the birthing experience they were hoping for and bonding does not happen immediately for most mothers. It can take up to three months to truly bond with your baby.

Alice now has a beautiful baby boy too and although she had some anxiety and fear around what it would be like the second time around, she had no expectations. She was prepared to be curious about how her baby would arrive, what the bonding and breastfeeding would be like and how she would feel afterwards. Alice did have a natural birth and she did manage to breastfeed and by using the skills and strategies we devised together in therapy, she managed to avoid post-natal anxiety.

Expectations of Support
One of the most common problems in relationships when a baby comes along is the disappointment and resentment that mothers feel towards their partners who do not live up to their expectations of support.

Dave and Anne came to see me after Anne had been diagnosed with post-natal anxiety. Their daughter was eight weeks old and they were really struggling to cope with the new addition to their family. They described their relationship before their daughter was born as loving and supportive. They believed they really knew each other well and that they had made the decision to have a baby, as it was something they both really wanted. They both had successful careers before their baby was born and they both had very supportive families.

Anne had a few expectations around motherhood, but they were both open to the experience and felt prepared for their baby. Anne had never experienced any anxiety or depression in the past and was feeling very out of control with the anxiety she was experiencing after her baby was born.

Dave felt helpless and did not know how to help Anne, in fact he felt like he was experiencing mild depression. It is not uncommon for men to experience post-natal anxiety and or depression – the statistics show that one in ten men in Australia suffer from this (PANDA, 2017).

We began working together and discovered that because Anne had always been so capable in everything she had undertaken, she had struggled from the day her baby was born to ask for help. *(The common humanity or shared understanding of this is that we are all human and we all need help at times in life in order to cope and share the burden of our experience.)* She also had an expectation that Dave would know what to do and how to help as he had always been there for her. *(This is a common shared belief amongst couples that have been together in supportive relationships.)* He always knew what to do when she needed him in the past.

Anne had not expected to feel so overwhelmed by the responsibility of being the main caregiver and protector of her daughter and was constantly second-guessing herself.

She was fearful something was going to happen to her baby *(this is another example of a shared human fear as every mother at some point feels overwhelmed by the thought that their baby depends on them for survival)*. If Dave did try and help her with the baby she would criticise everything he did. He felt like he was damned if he helped and damned if he didn't.

By the time she received her diagnosis of post-natal anxiety, Anne's unhelpful thoughts had run away with her and she was living in a constant state of fear. We worked on some practical ways to help with her anxiety and between us we worked out some strategies for Anne to be able to ask Dave for exactly what she wanted help with and how she wanted him to do things so that her anxiety did not overwhelm her. Dave also learnt to reassure Anne instead of getting despondent or irritated with her irrational thought process. He also worked on his own feelings of *"not being good enough"* for his wife and daughter. This feeling was the main contributor to his depression. Thankfully, Anne and Dave are now embracing the experience of being parents and have new strategies to deal with any anxiety or depression that may interfere with their experience as parents.

Anne's advice to any new mother is: *"Ask for help even if you don't think you need it and remember people can't read your mind. Let them know exactly what you need help with instead of setting them up to fail! I felt so alone in my head. The reality was my husband was also feeling so alone and all he needed was me to let him know how he could share the experience and how he could help."*

*

By gaining an understanding of common humanity or the shared human experience we are able to step into the understanding that we are not alone. Other mothers experience similar thoughts and feelings and our unrealistic expectations are also part of being human. We can normalise some of the difficulties we experience in motherhood. Believe it or not, mothers are not super human – we are human, and we do make mistakes. We are not perfect, but we can strive to be *"good enough"* in our own unique way.

Are the expectations you have created for yourself and those around you realistic or are they expectations that should be created for super-humans? Take time to notice your humanity and your imperfections. Embrace them because they are what connects you to the world around you and allows you to be who you are. Step out of the shadows of unrealistic expectations and into the light of reality by accepting your common humanity. It brings more joy in life once you accept it!

Chapter 9

Shadow Emotions

"The reason we suffer from our emotions is not because of the emotion itself, but because of our resistance to that particular emotion."
– Teal Swan

Although we are emotional beings designed to experience the full range of comfortable and uncomfortable emotions, we have lost the ability to deal with emotional suffering. We have done a great job learning how to suppress emotions. As a result, we have forgotten how to self-soothe, regulate and accept our emotions. Becoming a mother is an emotional rollercoaster, so it is no surprise that the *third shadow* of motherhood identified in my research and working with mothers is *"emotional suffering"*.

This art that we have mastered of suppressing emotions has resulted in what I like to refer to as the Volcano Effect: the more you supress emotions – especially the uncomfortable ones – the stronger their intensity. Eventually they cannot be suppressed any longer and the volcano erupts in a myriad of emotions, more often than not resulting in anxiety, depression, anger or a combination of all three! The more we avoid or try and ignore emotions the stronger they become and the more emotional distress and suffering we experience. In order to deal with difficult emotions, we need to find ways to accept the emotions for what they are – part of the human experience. We need to find ways to soothe and reassure ourselves that these emotions will pass. Deepak Chopra says, *"Instead of resisting any emotion, the best way to dispel it is to enter it fully, embrace it and see through your resistance."*

Some of the most difficult and distressing emotions that mothers have reported to cause the most suffering in motherhood are anger, resentment, guilt, anxiety, fear, sadness, exhaustion and internal conflict or angst. These are difficult emotions to deal with in life in general, let alone in motherhood, especially when there is an expectation that this is the *"happiest time of a woman's life"*. It is not easy for most mothers to talk about these emotions without feeling judged and judging themselves as *"bad mothers"*. Let me share with you some of the examples that mothers have given me over the years that have been the source of their emotional distress.

Anger and Resentment

The feelings of anger and resentment often come from the feeling of injustice that husbands, partners and everyone around them still have their identity, social life and working careers. Accepting identity loss (as we have discussed previously in this book) and finding a new sense of purpose, from a career woman to a mother, is a difficult change to make. The resentment and anger triggered by this is unexpected both from the mother herself and from the unsuspecting partner, husband, friend or family member. As one mother stated: *"If I look back on that whole experience I was extremely angry, I was horrible and, I cringe about it now, but I felt resentful of my husband going to work."*

Anger and resentment may also arise as a result of motherhood disappointment when expectations do not match reality – the gap. Expectations of birthing, bonding, breastfeeding, sex of the child, support from others and the mother's own ability to cope are just some of the unmet expectations that can result in feelings of anger and resentment.

Guilt

Guilt is a very strong emotion in the motherhood experience and often one that many mothers do not admit to feeling. It brings with it the dreaded emotion of shame. The guilt manifests in many forms, but a common theme for feelings of guilt arises from not enjoying the experience of motherhood as much as mothers should be or are expected to be. Alex was a lovely mum who was racked with guilt from the moment she found out she was pregnant. Although she wanted to be a mum and her pregnancy was planned, she did not like being pregnant and felt guilty for saying anything. Her sisters, her mother and everyone else she knew had loved being pregnant and said it was one of the best experiences. She was very distressed that she would not bond with her baby and spent her whole pregnancy pretending to be enjoying it and putting on a brave face to meet the expectations of the outside world. The guilt she felt and the shame that came with it caused her to constantly doubt her ability to be a mother and set her up for a difficult emotional journey even after the baby was born.

Several other mothers I have worked with in the past who have experienced perinatal anxiety and depression have spoken about their guilt around not being able to speak out when they were struggling to cope, wishing they had done so sooner so that they could have enjoyed the early experience of being a mother more. As one mother said to me: *"But I didn't know that I was suffering from anxiety at that point until it came to a head. A lot of it was the guilt associated with not getting a diagnosis, support and medication earlier."*

There is also a lot of guilt that comes up for mothers who have to go back to work and leave their babies and for mothers who choose to spend time doing things for themselves. There is a belief that you should want to spend every minute of the day with your baby. Jane was one of those mothers who, prior to having her baby, led an active physical life at the gym, walking with friends and playing netball. She stopped all of this when her baby was born and came to see me when she realised she was beginning to resent her baby for taking away her physical life. *"I feel guilty all the time if I'm not spending time with my baby and I know it is not valid guilt but I feel like it should be."*

Anxiety/Fear

All mothers experience feelings of anxiety and fear at some stage in their motherhood experience. It is natural to experience some anxiety, as we know that anxiety is the fear of the unknown and – as we have already established – becoming a mother is unpredictable and unknown! If anxiety is ignored or avoided it increases in intensity and may result in a more unhelpful and debilitating form of anxiety that requires a diagnosis of perinatal anxiety and requires treatment in the form of therapy and medication.

There are many different triggers for anxiety in motherhood and there is a correlation between lack of sleep and increased levels of anxiety. As one mother said: *"In my pregnancy when I wasn't sleeping I would get really anxious and it was linked in together. The more I didn't sleep the more anxious I would get. I really wanted to sleep but my body just wouldn't let me. I started becoming anxious about going to sleep and what that night would be like and pacing up and down in the middle of the night."*

As we all know, anxiety is a fear-driven response and having a baby to be responsible for creates a certain amount of fear in everyone. There is a little person who requires you to ensure they survive and that you survive to take care of them. Some mothers relate their anxiety to the fear of their baby or themselves getting sick. One mother reported to me that the anxiety around this left her paralysed and unable to function: *"My biggest anxiety issue was my baby was going to get sick or something was going to happen to me. We tried to go away on holiday and my baby got sick. I spent the whole weekend paralysed – my husband had to do everything, I just couldn't."*

Mothers are often distressed when their babies are crying or showing signs of discomfort and this can also be a source of anxiety. On more than one occasion mothers have told me that they have felt so anxious when their baby cries, when the baby is experiencing discomfort or will not go to sleep. The anxiety triggers a feeling of helplessness and they feel overwhelmed and out of control.

Sadness

Apart from the expected baby blues in the days after birth, mothers often report feelings of sadness that overwhelms them. Sometimes this leads to depression and results in them disconnecting from the true experience of motherhood. We are all led believe that motherhood is supposed to be a "happy" time, so when feelings of sadness arise most mothers try and suppress or deny the feelings and give themselves a hard time for feeling sad. In order to fully embrace our emotions of joy and true happiness we have to be prepared to accept uncomfortable emotions such as sadness.

Motherhood is no exception. With the combination of hormonal changes, body changes and identity changes, it is to be expected that at times during this transition to motherhood we will experience some uncomfortable as well as comfortable emotions. We are emotional beings and part of being human is the ability to feel and express the full range of emotions. Statistically, one in five mothers in Australia are presenting with perinatal anxiety and/or depression (PANDA, 2017). Although a proportion of this presentation is clinical and requires a diagnosis and treatment, there is a large proportion of anxiety and depression that is a result of suppressed emotion: emotion that has not been acknowledged and leads to a feeling of being overwhelmed. A mother's response to this overwhelmed feeling can cause them to shutdown, disconnect and doubt their ability to cope.

Exhaustion

No one can prepare a mother for the level of exhaustion and lack of sleep she will encounter during pregnancy and in the early months after their child is born. Most mothers experience exhaustion that they were unprepared for. The exhaustion may be due to lack of sleep, broken sleep, or the need to be productive and be able to cope. The feelings of exhaustion often make it difficult for them to be truly attuned to the needs of their babies. When they are exhausted and their babies cry, their ability to cope diminishes further. As one mother stated, *"I would wake up and there's a little person screaming for you. You are just exhausted – it didn't seem so lovely and rosy. I had never been in a situation where I was truly sleep deprived before, so I was very under prepared for that constant broken sleep."*

We all know that when we don't get enough sleep we are more than likely to be over-emotional, easily irritated and have less ability to focus and cope with everyday tasks. Here is one mother's view of this: *"I just didn't realise how hard things can be when you are so tired. Even easy tasks are so much harder when you are tired. The sleep thing was one of my biggest challenges."*

I have found with most mothers in therapy that there is this assumption that as lack of sleep is part of motherhood they should just be able to cope with it. They should be able to do everything and more! Part of this assumption and expectation comes from society and also from the mothers themselves. This results in them not giving themselves permission to rest and take care of themselves. As a consequence, their physical and emotional health is compromised and so is their connection to their baby. Sometimes, even when mothers reach out for support from others including professionals, they are met with judgement and disapproval. As one mother reported: *"I went to the doctor and she said there was nothing she could do for me ... so I rang the midwife again. I said, 'I need help, I don't think you understand'. She said, 'Oh, we can refer you to the psychiatrist', and that freaked me out and I said, 'I am not crazy I just haven't slept!'"*

Apart from feeling exhausted from lack of sleep, mothers often talk about their frustration over their babies not sleeping and the comparisons they make with other people's babies. This is evident in this mother's statement *"They had babies that would sleep and I was battling to get my baby to sleep and we were up all night. My husband and I would take shifts at night just so we could get some sleep. One of us would hold the baby half the night and then the other would take over, so I was often up half the night. I guess I was always frustrated and questioned what I was doing wrong and why my baby didn't sleep. It's crazy how few mums share their frustration over this for fear of being judged! But it's really hard to deal with and takes a toll on your relationship with your partner and your baby."*

Internal Conflict/Emotional Struggle

There is a common theme that mothers present with that creates internal conflict, an inner turmoil or an emotional struggle. These feelings are often a result of the expectation mothers have of themselves to be organised, productive and to achieve all they did before becoming mothers and more. This internal struggle is centred on the lack of ability to prioritise tasks and achieve as much as they used to. As stated by one mother: *"I always thought I was good at prioritising what was important and what was not important. But I think I did not manage that very well when I was struggling. I could never do anything; it was always hard to get things done. It was always an internal battle; everything seemed hard. Nothing ever flowed for me and my baby like it seemed to for everyone else."*

Although there is some expectation that motherhood will be challenging, most mothers say that they underestimated the challenges and they were much "harder" to accept. Most mothers are not prepared for the difficult parts of mothering, such as the "battle" of trying to get their babies to sleep during the day. *"When you have a baby that is screaming every time you want to put them down for a nap, it's always a battle, it's difficult. I don't think I had a really good notion of what the difficult parts would be like. I certainly was not prepared for it. I knew that mothers had challenges but I didn't think it would be that hard."*

*

This chapter has focused on some of the emotional suffering that can be experienced during motherhood. The reason for focusing on this emotional suffering is not to paint a gloomy picture of motherhood, but more so to normalise some of these difficult emotions and to encourage and allow mothers to be more open and talk about their emotional challenges without being judged or judging themselves. It is also to bring awareness to the fact that part of being human is to experience comfortable and uncomfortable emotions. We need to learn how to accept all the emotions we experience if we are to fully embrace and enjoy life.

Chapter 10

True Emotions

"The present moment is filled with joy and happiness. If you are attentive, you will see it."
– Thich Nhat Hanh

Most people find it incredibly challenging to accept their emotions and express them in a healthy way. Mothers are often fearful of expressing "negative" emotions or uncomfortable emotions, as they fear that this may impact their relationship with their baby. The reality is that unexpressed and suppressed emotions cause more distress and disconnection. The *third step* to master the skill of self-compassion and get out of the shadows and into the true motherhood experience is *mindfulness*. Mindfulness allows us to accept painful feelings and thoughts and gives us the ability to be aware of our experiences in the present moment with clarity and balance. Mindfulness allows us to neither ignore nor fixate on negative life experiences and fosters a flexible thought process that allows for a non-judgemental acceptance of self.

Mindfulness will offer mothers the ability to accept painful emotions and provide the ability to self-soothe in times of suffering. It is also an essential practice that helps mothers be more attuned to their babies and fosters healthy secure attachment. Mindfulness is one of the most crucial skills that not only mothers but everyone in society should be mastering. It has been proven to change the brain, reduce emotional suffering, increase wellbeing and make life more meaningful.

Science of Mindfulness

Mindfulness has been around for centuries and has its origin in early Buddhist traditions. Over the years more and more research and interest in the practice of mindfulness has resulted in it becoming a regular topic in daily conversation. There has been a lot of research into the effects that mindfulness has on the brain. It is evident from many studies that mindfulness leads to positive emotional, psychological and physical wellbeing. In order to understand why it has these positive outcomes we need to understand a bit about neurobiology and neuroplasticity. Neuroplasticity is the ability of the brain to change and adapt over time. Our brains have the ability to reorganise and adapt to function more efficiently and effectively. When we are challenged with a new task that we accomplish our brain takes note of it and often makes new connections or pathways to assist in completing the task next time.

There are numerous studies that provide evidence from a neurobiological perspective that the practice of mindfulness increases areas of the brain that are important for cognitive functioning such as attention and decision making, as well as learning and memory. Mindfulness also impacts brain systems that control emotion regulation and self-awareness. Recent studies have shown that the areas of the brain that are associated with cognitive functioning were more active after regular mindfulness practice. There is also evidence that the area of the brain that handles stress and strong emotions was less active (Siegel, 2017). As a result of this, people who practise mindfulness have a greater ability to regulate their emotions. They are less reactive and their performance and focus on tasks improves, along with their ability to connect to others in relationship.

What mindfulness is not ...

A way to control your mind

We cannot control our minds. It is the true nature of our minds to be thinking, judging and in a state of automatic mental activity. Once we are able to be curious and pay attention to our minds, we are able to notice how thoughts come and go. We are able to differentiate between thoughts that are true and thoughts that do not need our attention.

Zoning out or escaping

This is in fact the opposite of mindfulness. If you are zoned out or spaced out you are in a state of mindlessness not mindfulness. Mindfulness is about tuning into and connecting with what is going inside us and around us in the here and now or present moment. In fact, mindfulness is not about doing, it's more to do with being – being in the moment.

Simply paying attention

We all know how to pay attention to something, but mindfulness is not just paying attention to your mind. It is the ability to pay attention in a curious, kind way and without judgement to your present moment experience.

A pleasant, peaceful experience

Although the regular practice of mindfulness brings a sense of peace and relaxation into our worlds, the reality is that pleasant outcomes from mindfulness are not always guaranteed. There may be times when the practice of mindfulness brings up difficult and uncomfortable thoughts and feelings. We need to be prepared to accept all the experiences that mindfulness brings us. Mindfulness does however provide us with the ability to notice these difficult experiences and accept them rather than avoid them and increase our resistance to them.

About perfection and being who we are not

The aim of mindfulness is not to turn us all into Zen-like creatures who are perfect and live a life of peace and relaxation. Although that would be a nice thought, the reality is none of us are perfect and perfection is not a reality. Our reality is what is right now in the present moment and mindfulness helps us accept reality and accept ourselves for who we are.

Getting rid of painful thoughts and feelings

We cannot get rid of thoughts and feelings; in fact, we cannot even choose our thoughts and feelings. We can choose how we react and respond to our thoughts and feelings and that is where mindfulness is invaluable. Mindfulness allows us not only to accept our thoughts, feelings and sensations with curiosity and compassion, it also creates a space for us to slow down our automatic responses and choose how we are going to react and respond.

A religion

Although the origins of mindfulness are associated with early Buddhist traditions and beliefs, mindfulness is not a religion. It can help us feel connected on a spiritual level, but it is not aligned with any specific culture or religion. It is an innate human experience that taps into our natural abilities of awareness and compassion. In earlier civilisations mindfulness was second nature, but in our busy, materialistic society today it is now an essential skill that we need to re-learn.

Difficult to learn

As I mentioned, mindfulness is based on our natural abilities of curiosity, awareness, acceptance and compassion. It is not difficult to do. But it does require practice and a conscious daily commitment to be mindful. Over time, mindfulness does become a form of second nature, much like it was for our ancestors who had time to notice the world around them and the world inside them.

Only about meditation

There is a common misconception that mindfulness is just meditation. Meditation is a form of exercise for our minds to strengthen our mindfulness practice. Just as we choose physical exercise to strengthen our bodies and keep them in good working order, so too should we be using the practice of meditation to keep our minds in good working order.

A waste of time

In fact, it is the opposite! If you think you are too busy to practise mindfulness and make it part of your daily life you are basically saying that you are too busy to live a happy, healthy and meaningful life. The reality is if you are not practising mindfulness and have not mastered the art of living in the present moment then you are more than likely living in the past and the future. There is strong evidence to suggest that if this is what you are doing on a day-to-day basis you are wasting more time and energy than you can afford to. You will probably not be very focused and efficient. Mindfulness teaches us how to be in the present moment. It gives us the ability to use all our energy to focus on what is really going on in the here and now, not what has happened or what might happen. Mindfulness is a time-saver, not a time waster.

Mindfulness is ...

"Mindfulness is the basic human ability to be fully present, aware of where we are and what we're doing, and not overly reactive or overwhelmed by what's going on around us." (Mindful, 2014)

Mindfulness is something that we all possess, but as life has become so busy and technology has become our greatest distraction we have lost the ability to tap into this natural skill. Our ability to live a more mindful life and be fully immersed in meaningful experiences depends on our commitment and regular practise of mindfulness.

Mothers who master the art of living more mindfully find not only the transition to motherhood more enjoyable, but they have the ability to regulate their emotions, soothe themselves in times of suffering and be more available to connect with their babies.

How to begin being mindful

Most of our emotional suffering and distress is caused when our minds are focused on unhelpful thoughts and feelings of the past or future. In order to allow ourselves to step back into the present moment we need to find an anchor or a focus point that allows the brain to let go of the unhelpful thoughts or feelings it has attached its attention to.

The easiest way for us to come back in the present moment is to focus on our breathing. Our breath is constant; it is automatic from the time we are born until the time we die. The easiest form of mindfulness practice is to simply allow yourself to focus on your breath – noticing that as you breathe in you can feel the cool air passing through your nostrils and as you breathe out you can notice the warm air passing out through your nose. Even simply saying the words, *"I'm breathing in ... I'm breathing out,"* brings focused attention to your breath and allows the mind to settle and the body to relax.

Try it for yourself. Take five deep breaths in and out, notice the air passing in and out of your nose and say these words to yourself: *"I'm breathing in ... I'm breathing out"*.

As Amit Ray (2015) so aptly quotes: *"Breath is the finest gift of nature. Be grateful for this wonderful gift."*

Introducing mindfulness into your life can be as simple as doing your daily tasks, chores or work in a mindful way. This is often the first element of mindfulness I introduce to mothers who are feeling overwhelmed.

Lucy was one mother who found that the simple daily practices of mindfulness changed her whole experience of being a new mum. When Lucy came to see me, she was very stressed and not really enjoying being a mum – she felt like she was never achieving anything, she was very distracted and did not feel like she was very bonded to her baby. Lucy was also struggling with some difficult emotions. She felt guilty for not enjoying time with her baby, she was anxious that her baby might be sensing her stress and she felt sad that she wasn't able to cope like she had thought she would.

After completing a simple exercise of what she was doing on a day-to-day basis, it became evident that Lucy was very caught up in her head about what she hadn't done (the past) and should be doing (the future). This was causing her to lose focus on any task she was trying to attempt. For example, she would be folding the washing whilst her baby was sleeping but instead of finishing that she would start tidying the lounge room or unpacking the dishwasher. Then her baby would wake up and she hadn't completed anything. Apart from feeling frustrated that her baby had woken up before she had finished she would also be annoyed with herself for not achieving some basic chores.

The cycle would continue, and by the end of the day Lucy would feel that she was not a good mother, not a good wife and would give herself a hard time comparing herself to other mothers who could do it all! Lucy agreed to try some mindfulness practices but was concerned that she would not have enough time in the day to do them. We started with simply choosing one task that she could do mindfully each day – it could be something as simple as folding the washing or having a mindful shower. Folding the washing mindfully for Lucy meant noticing what she was folding – the item of clothing, the colours, the texture, the smell of the washing powder on the fabric. If her mind wandered she would re-focus on what she could see, smell, hear and feel.

Slowly but surely, Lucy introduced mindfulness to all her daily tasks, including mindfully feeding her baby, mindfully bathing or dressing her baby, mindfully eating and mindfully showering. Lucy and I tracked her progress for six weeks and her levels of anxiety and stress decreased, she reported more joy in her motherhood experience and felt more attuned and bonded to her baby. The difficult emotions she was experiencing were still there, but she was able to notice them, accept them and be more compassionate and understanding towards herself. If you do not already practise any mindfulness give yourself a challenge and try and choose one task/activity/chore that you do each day and see if you can do it mindfully.

Using mindfulness to overcome painful/difficult emotions in motherhood

As I have already mentioned in the previous chapter, there are many emotions experienced in motherhood and dealing with them is challenging, especially when they are painful or difficult emotions. In order to use mindfulness to help alleviate the suffering caused by these emotions, the first step we have to take is to be able to notice the emotions and bring awareness to them instead of trying to deny them or suppress them. Most of our emotions emerge as physical sensations before we actually have the ability to name them as emotions. If you are not familiar with the felt sense or sensation of different emotions in your body, you may like to start by trying this mindfulness exercise to bring awareness to and to label or name the emotion:

Sit in a comfortable position and notice the ground beneath you.

Take three breaths in and out allowing yourself to anchor your attention to your breath.

Bring your attention to your heart region and, if it feels comfortable for you, place your hand over your heart.

Find your breath around your heart and feel your chest move up and down as you breathe.

If your mind wanders bring your attention back to the sensation of your breathing.

After a few minutes try and recall a difficult emotion you are experiencing or one you have experienced and the situation around it.

Name the emotion and expand your awareness and scan your body from head to toe and notice where you feel that emotion – where you sense tension or discomfort.

Bring your attention to the place in your body where you feel it the most and focus on your breath.

Breathe in and around the tension in your body and allow it to soften – allow the discomfort to be there – let it come and go.

With your hand on your heart focus on the breath and send some love and comfort to yourself – you may wish to use the words soften, allow, love.

Continue focusing on the breath and sending love and comfort to your painful emotion until you notice the intensity of the tension and discomfort reduces.

Bring your attention back to your hand on your heart and your breath. When you are ready slowly open your eyes.

The more practice you have at tuning into the sensations in your body that are associated with emotions the more you will be able to soothe yourself in difficult times, the more you will be able to regulate your emotions in the here and now. This mindfulness practice is a key element of dealing with difficult emotions, but it is also an excellent exercise to use to tune into the positive or helpful emotions that we experience. The more you understand the sensations in your body and realise that they are a guide to emotional wellbeing, the sooner you will be able to embrace the full spectrum of human emotions and live a more meaningful life.

The gift of mindfulness

Mindfulness is not only the most valuable gift you can give yourself, it is also the most important gift a mother can give her child. Your true presence in your child's life will foster a foundation of attunement, connection, validation and security. Attunement is the key element that allows a child to be truly seen, heard, felt and accepted. We cannot as mothers be attuned to our children if we are distracted by our thoughts, feelings and sensations. We cannot be attuned if we are living in the past or living in the future. We can only truly be attuned to our children if we are living in the present and this can only be achieved through the practice of mindfulness and living in the here and now. You have the ability to be a mindful mother and to offer your child the experience of feeling safe, loved and connected. This gift of mindfulness does not cost the earth, but it may save the earth!

Chapter 11

Change Challenge

"The secret to change is to focus all of your energy not on fighting the old but on building the new."
– Socrates

Change is challenging for most people and often brings with it some resistance. Learning to be more self-compassionate in order to make motherhood, our relationships and experiences in our lives more meaningful is challenging. But I believe any form of change is an opportunity for growth and development. As I mentioned earlier in this book, we are born with a natural care-giving system in place and, although we have no problem activating it for others, we seem to have a huge resistance in activating it for ourselves. As we come to the final chapters of this book I thought it would be a good time to explore the concept of change and some of the science behind change and how to choose to commit to the changes we are trying to make.

Alan Deutschman, the author of *Change or Die*, believes that although we all have the ability to change we rarely ever do. In fact, the odds are nine to one that, when faced with the dire need to change, we won't. The challenge that Deutschman proposes in his book is: change or die? If we are given the choice of life or death most of us would choose life. But what if you had to make difficult changes in how you think, feel, behave and live your life or you would die? What would your choice be then? Do you think you could make changes when change matters the most? When have you made changes in life and how successful have you been? What makes some changes easy to make and others almost impossible to make?

Choosing Change

The reality is most of us talk about making changes in our lives, but we never really choose to make the changes or commit to making the changes. One of the biggest motivators for change is the reward or benefit we hope to receive. What would the reward or benefit be if you were to commit to becoming a more self-compassionate mother? How would you feel about yourself? What impact would it have on your psychological, emotional and physical wellbeing? How would it benefit the relationship you have with your baby? What influence would it have on your child's attachment style? How would your child's experience of being mothered by a self-compassionate mother influence his/her future relationships?

By this stage you should be able to answer all those questions. There are enough benefits for you and your baby, let alone everyone else around you, to consider committing to make the change to practise self-compassion and make it an integral part of your everyday life. But the first major step in making any lasting change is to get yourself into the right frame of mind or mindset.

Change Mindset

Change can occur even when you feel "stuck" or when you have resistance to the change. But in order to embrace change you need to be purposeful in your approach, your attitude and your activities, otherwise you may just end up as one of the nine in ten that don't change! There are three key elements to creating a change mindset.

New hope

This involves finding belief in ourselves that we can make the change and then surrounding ourselves with people who believe in our ability to change – people who will inspire and motivate us to change. Creating a sense of hope that we can change is the greatest form of motivation and inspiration.

New skills

It takes a lot of repetition over time before new patterns of thinking and behaving become automatic and seem natural. Practise until you embrace the new way without even thinking about it. In order to make the changes to be more self-compassionate you need to commit to the regular practice until it becomes second nature.

New thinking

Continue to find new ways of thinking about yourself, your situation and your life. Ultimately, you will look at the world in a way that would have been so foreign to you if you had not made the changes and life will have more value and meaning.

Why is it that even though we spend hundreds of dollars every year trying to change and improve, we still fail to achieve our goals of change? The reason is not so much that we don't want to change but more so that we don't understand change. We don't realise what is involved in the process of change. It is not simply making a decision to do things differently, it needs to be a conscious commitment and choice to find ways to think, feel and act differently. We usually make two common mistakes when we try and motivate ourselves or others to change. We rely on fear factor or fact factor. Fear factor may work in some instances but often only for a brief time. Fact factor does not often work as we have this amazing ability to choose to be in denial of facts, even when we are well aware that they are true. Our biggest challenge is to understand *why* we need to change, *how* we need to change and to actually *do it*.

I believe that creating a positive mindset to change is one element of the change process. But in my time working not only with mothers but with all my clients, I have noticed that unless changes are made in all areas of life the change is not sustainable, which brings me to the next topic I am so passionate about: Therapeutic Lifestyle Changes or TLC's.

Therapeutic Lifestyle Changes

A lot of research has gone into determining which lifestyle changes are the most important to prevent mental health issues, avoid chronic diseases and foster lasting changes for overall wellbeing. Therapeutic Lifestyle Changes are cost effective, backed up by extensive research in neuroscience, counselling, and medicine. They are enjoyable, inexpensive, free from side-effects, and easily available. We can all do them and have a good time doing them, while we make ourselves healthier and happier and create mindsets that are more self-compassionate.

There are eight key TLC's that have been widely researched and proven to effectively create and manage change and increase both physical and psychological wellbeing (Walsh, 2011). They will no doubt come as no surprise to you. I hope by highlighting them in this book for mothers it will create an opportunity for you to incorporate them into your daily life, to assist you in becoming a more self-compassionate mother and help you create more meaningful experiences, not only in motherhood, but for the rest of your life.

TLC 1 – Exercise

We all know exercise is good for us, but do we do it? We are designed to move.

The author John Ratey Spark believes, *"It is unethical for any health professional to work with a client and fail to prescribe exercise."* And I agree! Exercise gets blood flowing to your brain and body. Exercise increases brain volume, is as effective as medication for mild depression and anxiety, it may prevent cancer, and slow down or even prevent Alzheimer's. Exercise is one of the best prescriptions for any psychological distress. The boost in *"feel good hormones"* we receive from exercise is like a dose of the best tonic in the world. Exercise helps us sleep better, which, as you will be well aware, is one of the major challenges during pregnancy and after your baby is born. We have more ability to regulate our emotions if we exercise on a regular basis and this is a valuable skill all mothers will appreciate.

I know for many pregnant mums or new mums exercise can be challenging, not only physically but also due to a lack of time. Any form of exercise that you choose to do including a gentle walk outside in the fresh air or walking in the water at the local pool is good enough – if you can achieve some form of exercise for thirty minutes three times a week you will immediately notice a difference.

TLC 2 – Nutrition

You are probably reading this and thinking here we go again – we know all this! But I am constantly surprised by the number of my clients who know all these basic nutritional facts, yet they still continue to take no notice. They wonder why they don't feel good about themselves or why they are so anxious, depressed or stressed. The basics are well known – avoid the whites (pasta, sugar, salt) and snack on only healthy food. Vegetarian and Mediterranean ways of eating have been proven to be effective for overall wellbeing. When you choose to become a mother, you also choose to provide nutritional support to a little person who depends on you to develop to their full potential. You will be well aware of foods you should and should not be eating whilst you are pregnant, breastfeeding and raising your child to be healthy and happy. If you are not sure of the best diet for you and your baby, please take the time to get some advice and give yourself and your baby the best opportunity to be happy and healthy. A balanced healthy diet promotes physical and mental wellbeing and brain development. It aids in reducing stress, anxiety and depression in mothers and promotes healthy development in babies who display higher levels of emotional regulation.

TLC 3 – Sleep

This is a challenging TLC for all mothers as we have already discussed earlier in this book that a lack of sleep and exhaustion was one of the major challenges that resulted in mothers experiencing emotional distress, depression and/or anxiety. Adequate rest is critical for our brain function and for the development of new neural networks. Vital hormones required for psychological health and wellbeing such as serotonin and dopamine are produced during the sleep cycle. A lack of sleep interrupts this process and it is no wonder mothers are at an increased risk of experiencing depression and anxiety.

There is a common misconception that we need all our sleep in one go for it to be adequate. But in fact, shorter, regular periods of sleep can be just as beneficial. I have found that most mothers will not give themselves permission to sleep when their babies sleep or if they are pregnant to allow themselves an afternoon nap. This is driven by the fear of not being productive and achieving enough, not being good enough and being viewed as "lazy". The reality is the more you give yourself permission to sleep when your baby sleeps and nap when you have the opportunity, the more likely you are to find more time. You will be more motivated to do all those tasks or chores you are trying to do when you are exhausted! Please give yourself permission to sleep when you can and when you need to. It is a basic human need and is an essential ingredient for enjoying the experience of being a mum.

TLC 4 – Relationships

We are all relational beings and being with others in a positive way helps deal with emotional distress and leads to feelings of connectedness and wellbeing. Healthy, positive relationships build longer telomeres, which are an essential element of our cells that determines how we age. Love is the foundation for health. Love and feeling an emotional connection to others encourages the production of *oxytocin* which is known as the *"love hormone"*. We are hard-wired from birth to seek out connection with others in order to thrive and survive. Neglect, rejection, isolation and loneliness have all been shown to have a significant impact on the brain causing it to shrink and become over-activated in areas such as the amygdala that trigger stress reactions and create a state of hyper arousal.

In fact, the quality of our relationships is one of the most important of all lifestyle factors in determining the quality of our lives. The dramatic effect of relationships on our wellbeing is grounded in the very design of our brain. The new research field of social neuroscience shows that we are hard-wired for empathy and intimacy. Our brains resonate with one another like tuning forks, picking up subtle emotional and social cues, enabling us to empathise with others, and to literally feel what they feel. In every relationship and in every interaction, we create an intimate brain-to-brain link-up. This neural link allows us to feel and affect the brain function of everyone we meet. We are not only parts of social networks but parts of neural networks.

Given this intimate link between our brains, it's no surprise that our relationships are so important and powerful and that we affect each other so dramatically.

As a mother there will be many relationships you will be required to focus on, the most important being the one with your baby. Try and make sure that the other relationships in your life are healthy and positive, as this will have a major influence on the type of relationship you have with your baby. Remember you deserve to be loved and appreciated. Don't settle for or invest your time in relationships that do not make you feel good about yourself. Being in healthy, loving relationships is one of the greatest gifts you can give not only to yourself but also to your baby.

TLC 5 – Cognitive Challenge
In order to make changes we need to challenge our brain, encourage new pathways to open up and provide an opportunity for the brain to get out of autopilot mode! Challenge your cognitive skills. Take a course, learn a language, learn a new instrument – basically do something different to create new neural networks. Uncertainty can be growth producing. *"Jiggle your synapses a bit"* and challenge thoughts and ideas that are contrary to your own. There are many simple cognitive challenges such as the Luminosity app and doing Sudoku or the crossword in the daily paper. You can even do the simplest of things on a daily basis such as wearing your watch on the opposite arm, choosing to drive or walk home a different way from work or the shops, or choosing to drink a cup of coffee or tea with your non-dominant hand.

All of these small tasks that we can do with our eyes closed are done on what I like to call autopilot. Your brain does not need to work hard to perform repetitive daily tasks. If you want to create new neural pathways and open up opportunities for change you need to get out of autopilot! It is probably worth mentioning here that constructive cognitive challenges do not include watching too much TV, spending too much time on social media, sitting for long periods of time or continuing repetitive routines.

TLC 6 – Relaxation

There are so many benefits to be gained from relaxation and recreation. When we allow ourselves to relax and let go we recreate, refresh and revitalise ourselves. It is important to bring in humour and playfulness into our relaxation and recreation element of life. Playfulness is built into our biology and is a source of natural wellbeing, happiness and self-worth. Think back to when you were a child – what did you love doing, how did you play and how did you feel when you were left to be free and make up your own games and stories? When was the last time you played like a child and laughed out loud with the wind in your hair and the sun on your face?

It is so sad that as we grow up most of us lose the ability to maintain a sense of playfulness in our lives. The only time you see adults giving themselves permission to play, laugh and have innocent fun is when there are children around. They somehow give themselves permission to play. When adults do let go and you see a mum or dad or grandparents playing with children it is a joy to watch their laughter and see the smiles on their faces. They forget about the world around them and immerse themselves in the experience. There are so many ways to relax and play and I encourage you to find time in your life to do this, especially as a mum. If you can play and have fun, you will be able to model that to your children. They will have the ability to experience the joy that relaxation and play can bring.

Relaxation can also be something as simple as spending time in nature on a daily basis. We are a part of nature and nature is a part of us. For the first time in history, we live divorced from nature, living in artificial environments. We spend hours each day immobile in front of television, mobile phones and computer screens. As a result of this we now have a new generation of psychological disorders: nature-deficit disorder, digital fog, technostress, techno-brain burnout and various technology-based addictions.

Fortunately for us, spending time in natural settings is healing and restorative. Natural settings can reduce symptoms of stress, depression, anxiety, ADHD and many more mental health issues. Patients in hospital rooms that overlook natural settings suffer less pain after surgery, require less pain medication, and leave hospital sooner. There is a simple prescription for wellbeing all around us in the form of nature. Take time to be in nature, sit under the trees in the park, watch the waves at the beach, walk in the sand, find your favourite spot in your garden and listen to the sound of nature all around you!

TLC 7 – Contribution & Service

"If giving weren't free, pharmaceutical companies could herald the discoveries of a stupendous new drug called give back instead of Prozac." (Post and Newmark, 2007).

We were not designed to live for ourselves alone. We are social beings designed to be part of a community or tribe in order to survive and thrive. Service to others or *"giving back"* is not necessarily a sacrifice, but rather can benefit both the giver and receiver. People who volunteer more are happier and healthier and even live longer. Elderly volunteers who donate their time to assist students display improved intellectual abilities and better brain function. Generosity tends to lead to more generosity, and those who witness kind and caring behaviours are more likely to be kind and caring themselves. Generosity and service to others improves our psychological, physical and brain wellbeing. When people help others, they themselves are helped and they tend to end up happier and healthier. Contribution and service to others has long been considered an essential element of a life well lived. Now they can also be considered essential elements of a healthy life.

As the Dalai Lama puts it: *"If you are going to be selfish, be wisely selfish – which means to love and serve others, since love and service to others brings rewards to oneself that would otherwise be unachievable."*

TLC 8 – Spirituality

Religion and spirituality are vitally important to most people and 90% of the world's population engages in religious and spiritual practices. For the other 10%, some appreciation of the *"big picture"* – the size and wonder of the universe – is invaluable.

Religion and spirituality are especially important in coping with emotional stress and illness as they provide a foundation for help and support. These religious and spiritual practices are especially effective if they emphasise qualities such as love and forgiveness, rather than focusing on themes of guilt, sin, and punishment. Mentally, people with regular religious-spiritual practices are less likely to suffer from psychological difficulties such as anxiety and depression or drug and alcohol abuse. They are also likely to be psychologically healthier and happier, to be more resilient, and to have better relationships and marriages.

One of the most remarkable of all research findings is that people who attend religious or spiritual meetings weekly tend to live an average of seven years longer than those who don't. Take the time to think about your own spiritual beliefs and practices and how you can make them a focus of your attention to live a more meaningful life and reap the benefits of this TLC!

Change your mindset and lifestyle to make change last

So, in summary, if you are going to choose to make the changes to become more self-compassionate you need to use the Therapeutic Lifestyle Changes as a vehicle for changing your mindset to take care of yourself. Eat right, get enough sleep, drink plenty of water and engage in regular physical activity. Ensure you have a healthy mind and body through activities like yoga, taking a short walk, going to the gym or doing activities that will enhance both your physical and mental health. Take time to relax and play.

No matter how hectic life gets, make time for yourself – even if it's just simple things like reading a good book or listening to your favourite music. Reach out for support when you need it. Accepting help from supportive friends, family and professionals can improve your ability to make the changes you need to make in order to enjoy your experience of being a mother.

Chapter 12

Meaningful Motherhood

"In giving birth to our babies, we may find that we give birth to new possibilities within ourselves."
– Myla and Jon Kabat-Zinn

Learning the art of self-compassion provides a platform for a unique, meaningful motherhood experience. In this chapter I would like to summarise the *"shadows of motherhood"* we have explored and look at the *"three ways"* self-compassion can be used to alleviate the emotional and psychological distress that lurks in these shadows. It goes without saying that by understanding your own needs as a mother and finding love, acceptance and compassion for yourself you will be more attuned to your baby. There is more opportunity for him/her to have an experience of secure attachment and to feel safe and loved.

Let's take a look at key messages and knowledge that this book has highlighted:

Accepting and creating a new identity

In the beginning we discussed the need for us to accept the fact that we need to recreate our identity when we decide to become a mother. Being prepared to recreate your identity and find meaning in your new identity as a mother is critical to having a meaningful motherhood experience. Preparing for the transition to motherhood and the change in your identity is one of the secrets to embracing the change and becoming the mother that you truly want to be. Accepting, validating and encouraging yourself are key aspects to recreating your identity. Try this loving kindness meditation to help you connect to your baby and accept your new identity with love and compassion.

Loving-kindness Meditation for Mothers

Start with loving-kindness for yourself as a mother or mother-to-be.

Sit comfortably and bring your attention to your breath.

Place your hand over your heart and repeat the following phrases:

May I be filled with love and kindness.

May I treat myself with kindness.

May I be safe and healthy.

May I live with ease.

Bring your baby to mind

If you are a mother-to-be, bring to your awareness to your baby growing within.

If you are a mother, bring your baby to mind, hold your baby in your arms or look at your baby sleeping. Share the loving-kindness with your baby and in a gentle tone repeat the following phrases:

May my baby be surrounded with love and kindness.

May I respond to my baby with kindness.

May my baby be safe and healthy

May my baby live with ease.

Try and connect with your baby and feel the loving-kindness between you and feel the meaning in the phrases you are repeating. Notice if your mind wanders and bring it gently back without judgement and continue the meditation.

Now bring you and your baby to mind.

As you move your attention to the connection between you and your baby gently repeat the following phrases:

May we be surrounded with love and kindness.

May we respond to each other with kindness.

May we be safe and healthy.

May we live with ease.

As you experience this sense of connection between you and your baby, notice how you feel about yourself in this moment. Connect with this new identity of being a mother. Feel love and kindness towards yourself and your baby as you step into this unique relationship of unconditional love and acceptance.

The Myths of Motherhood

Like any major life transition there are many myths and misconceptions around the experience of motherhood that have been passed down through generations. Some myths and stories can be helpful and make us question our values and beliefs about the world around us. But there are many myths if taken literally that can be unhelpful. Myths can result in us moving away from reality and trying to create experiences that are unrealistic. We are all searching for the magic formula that will make us *"perfect mothers"* and will produce *"perfect children"* but the reality is there is no such formula and no such reality. Be mindful of the myths that may be influencing you as a mother and question how useful they might be in making your motherhood experience meaningful. Create your own unique story of your journey through motherhood and find your own meaning in the story.

The Importance of Attachment

Our experience of our relationship with our primary caregiver determines whether or not we develop a secure or insecure attachment style. Regardless of your own experience of being cared for and your own attachment style you have the ability as a mother to choose to provide a care environment for your child that will offer them the chance of developing a secure attachment style. Secure attachment provides us with the ability to be more emotionally regulated and to enter into and sustain meaningful relationships in our adult life. Secure attachment provides the foundation for respectful, loving and trustful relationships. As a mother there are some very simple things you can do to foster a sense of safety and love for your child. Show your baby warmth and understanding on a regular basis. Be tuned in and mindfully focused on the needs of your child, try and reduce your child's exposure to stress and trauma. Learn how to self-soothe your own uncomfortable emotions and model healthy emotional regulation to your baby. Remember the three most basic steps in creating a sense of safety and love for your baby: hug your baby often, use a gentle tone of voice and make eye contact every time you interact with your child. Remember that secure human attachment cannot be made through a haze of technology. Your attachment to your electronic devices such as your phone is one of society's biggest challenges in ensuring secure attachment in children. Please be mindful and notice if technology is interfering with your ability to connect to your child and be fully attuned to their needs.

Self-compassion

Even if you had the ability to be self-compassionate and take care of yourself before becoming a mother it is a known fact that most mothers are unable to continue this practice once they have their children. There is this deep-seated sense of responsibility that comes with being a mother that makes us choose to put ourselves last. We meet the needs of our children and those around us before allowing ourselves permission to have our own needs met. Being self-compassionate does not mean we are being selfish or self-centred. It means that we accept, respect and care about ourselves and know what we need to be able to be more available to meet the needs of our children and other loved ones. As you move towards making self-compassion a conscious focus in your life you may like to consider using a daily mantra or affirmation, one that encourages you and reminds you that you deserve to be cared for, accepted and loved. Here are a few that some of my clients have used in the past, but you may like to change the words so that you connect with and believe what you are saying:

I love and accept myself as I am right now.

I am loveable.

I deserve love, kindness and compassion.

I have a warm and caring heart.

I am confident in my individuality.

I am exactly who I need to be in this moment.

I am a beautiful person.

In times of difficulty and suffering you may like to practise using a self-compassion break which allows us to step into the practice of showing genuine love and understanding of our own pain and suffering.

Self-compassion break

Bring your focused attention to the difficult thoughts, feelings or sensations you are experiencing, place your hand on your heart or gently hug yourself and repeat the following phrases:

This is a moment of suffering.

Suffering is part of life.

May I be kind to myself.

May I give myself the compassion I need.

Self-kindness versus self-judgement

In order to be a more self-compassionate mother I invited you to consider stepping out of the shadow of self-judgement into the light of self-kindness. I hope by the time you are reading this last chapter you have found ways to speak kindly to yourself and treat yourself the way you would treat someone you love and respect. Remember to notice the unhelpful voice in your head – that inner critic – quieten it down and find a new way of speaking to yourself with a gentle, caring tone. Reality-check the judgements you have of yourself. Notice your positive qualities and strengths on a daily basis. Affirm and encourage yourself to step into being the beautiful, unique mother you are or will be. Live your life in accordance with your true core values.

Common humanity versus unmet expectations

This element of self-compassion encourages us to accept the fact that we are human, we are not perfect, we make mistakes and we fail. Becoming a mother is filled with not only your own expectations but also expectations from your family, friends and society. Choose wisely the expectations you set for yourself and your children. Take time to reality check them and notice where they have come from. Aim to be a *"good enough"* mother, not a perfect mother. If you are a good enough mother 60% of the time you are doing a lot better than most mothers out there who claim to be perfect! We all know that the reality portrayed on social media is a far cry from living reality. Don't get caught up in the comparisons of perfection. Rather, choose to be a realist and accept each moment of your journey through motherhood for what it is, not what it should or could be.

Mindfulness versus emotional suffering

The third element of self-compassion is not only the key to mastering the ability to be self-compassionate, it is also the essential ingredient in living a meaningful life. It will allow you to feel a deep sense of connection not only to your baby but also to the world around you. Hopefully after reading Chapter 10 and trying some of the practical day-to-day mindfulness activities, you are becoming aware of how much more enjoyable day-to-day life can be when we immerse ourselves fully in the moment-to-moment experience.

In my own personal journey to become more mindful, I catch myself on a day-to-day basis feeling more and more connected to the beautiful world of nature and all the joy it brings with it. I have also noticed the joy and connection that a simple smile and conscious eye contact brings to those around me. By allowing myself to see who I truly am, I have been able to make others around me feel seen and heard. If you haven't already started making mindfulness a daily practice, please try to. It will bring you more joy in life and will undoubtedly make your motherhood experience more meaningful. As I have already stated a few times in this book, the greatest gift you can give your child is the gift of being truly seen, acknowledged and accepted so that they can feel safe and loved.

As I write the final chapter of this book, I am reflecting on my journey up until this moment and I am overwhelmed with gratitude for so many reasons. So I thought it might be an appropriate way to end our time together by spending the last few pages taking note of the importance of gratitude in making our lives meaningful, to spend a little time noticing what we are grateful for.

In my own journey to find the courage and belief in myself to write this book I have so many people and experiences to be grateful for. Without the supportive, loving, wise people who have encouraged me along the way and the amazing mothers I have worked with over the years, I would not have found the courage and knowledge to write this book. I am also incredibly grateful for the path that led me to understand and implement self-compassion in my life – it has been the greatest gift I have ever been given and one I hope you have decided to give yourself. As a mother or mother-to-be I am sure there are many things you can bring to mind that you are grateful for, that bring you joy in your life. Hold those feelings of gratitude and joy close to your heart, as they are what make life worth living and make the experience of life meaningful. There are many guided mindfulness meditations to help us deal with difficult thoughts and feelings, but I would like to end this book inviting you to also make time in your life to practise mindfulness that welcomes feelings of gratitude and joy in your body and mind.

Mindfulness meditation to welcome joy and gratitude

Bring something to mind that you are grateful or thankful for.

With your eyes closed or open welcome the sounds you can hear around you, notice your breath and the sensations you can feel in your body.

Welcome the feelings of gratitude and joy into your body (what you are grateful or thankful for about being a mother today, what has brought you joy today).

Allow the feelings of joy and gratitude to flow through your body, feel your heart warming and feel a warm glow spreading through your body, notice the smile inside you.

If any uncomfortable feelings arise, notice them, accept them and allow them to be there.

Then focus your attention on the feelings of gratitude and joy – allow them to engulf your whole body, wrapping it in a golden glow of light.

Stay in the feeling of warmth and light, focusing on the gratitude and joy.

When you are ready bring your attention back to your body, open and close your eyes a few times and affirm your intention to feel joy and gratitude throughout your day.

Final words

Becoming a mother is not for the faint hearted! I am presuming that those of you who have read this book are considering becoming a mother, are pregnant, are already a mother or are supporting a mother or mother-to-be. Whether your experience up until this point has been a very positive one or one filled with challenges and suffering, there is no time like now to decide to do things differently and adopt some of the changes I have suggested in this book.

There are many mothers who have journeyed with me either in individual counselling or in therapeutic groups who have found these simple steps invaluable in their motherhood experience. The changes they have chosen to make have not only impacted their motherhood experiences in the here and now but also improved their connection and attachment to their babies. The changes have also influenced their experiences of motherhood with future pregnancies and babies.

I am well aware that most of these strategies and tips you would have heard before but perhaps you may not have found the motivation or mindset to make the changes. My hope for you is that you take away at least three changes suggested in this book and commit to consistently trying them for a six or twelve week period. If you notice life, especially motherhood, becoming more meaningful and enjoyable, please continue to commit to the change. If you have any friends or other mothers who can join you in your quest to make motherhood more meaningful, create a group to encourage each other to be committed to the change.

*

We have arrived at the end of our journey together and I hope you have enjoyed it as much as I enjoyed writing it and sharing it with you! I hope that you have begun your journey of self-compassion and that you are now treating yourself with the same love, understanding and compassion that you give to others. If this book has made a difference to your motherhood experience and your connection to your child and other significant people in your life, please share it with others and together we can make a difference. My dream is for every mother to have a meaningful motherhood experience, free from emotional suffering and for every child to have the opportunity of feeling safe, loved and connected.

May your motherhood experience be a self-compassionate and meaningful one!

With gratitude and much love to all mothers!

Bibliography

This book was inspired and informed by the following resources:

Coates, R., Ayers, A., & De Visser, R. (2014). Women's experiences of post natal distress: a qualitative study. *BMC Pregnancy Childbirth, 14*(359). doi:10.1186/14671-2393-14-359

Cranswick, C. (2017). *Self-compassion: What meaning and role does it play in the lives of women who experience anxiety and depression in the perinatal period?* Retrieved from University of Notre Dame: https://researchonline.nd.edu.au/theses/154/

Duncan, L., Coatsworth, J., & Greenberg, M. (2009). A model of mindful parenting: implications for parent-child relationship and prevention research. *Clinical Child and family Psychology Review, 12*(3), 255-270. Retrieved from http://doi.org/10.1007/s10567-009-0046-3

Germer, C. (2009). *The mindful path to self-compassion.* New York: Guilford Publications.

Gilbert, P. (2009). *The Compassionate Mind.* London: Constable.

Gilbert, P. (2014). The origins and nature of compassion focused therapy. *British Journal of Psychology, 53,* 6-41. doi:10.1111/bjc.12043

Hall, P., & Wittkowski, A. (2006). An exploration of negative thoughts as a normal phenomenon after childbirth. *Journal of Midwifery & Women's Health, 51*(5), 321-330. Retrieved from http://www.medscape.com/viewarticle/544983_4

Harwood, K., McLean, N., & Durkin, K. (2007). First-time mothers expectations of parenthood: What happens when optimistic expectations are not matched by later experiences? *Developmental Psychology, 43*(1), 1-12.

Health, D. o. (2016, March 10). *Common Emotional Problems.* Retrieved from Women and Newborn Health Service: http://www.kemh.health.wa.gov.au/health/emotional_health/common_emotional_problems.htm

Hollis-Walker, L., & Colosimo, K. (2011). Mindfulness, self-compassion and happiness in non-meditators: a theoretcial and empirical examination. *Personality and Individual Differences, 50,* 222-227. Retrieved from http://www.sciencedirect.com/science/article/pii/S0191886910004769

Kaitz, M., Maytal, H., Devor, N., Bergman, L., & Mankuta, D. (2010). Maternal anxiety, mother-infant interactions, and infants' responses to challenge. *Infant Behavior and development, 33,* 136-148. doi:10.1016/j.infbeh.2009.12.003

Kauppi, C., Montgomery, P., Shaikh, A., & White, T. (2012). Post Natal Depression: When reality does not match expectations. In D. M. Castillo (Ed.), *Perinatal Depression* (pp. 55-80). In Tech. Retrieved from http://www.intechopen.com.books/perinatal-depression/postnatal-depression-when-reality-does-not-match-expectations

Lama, H. t. (1997). *The power of compassion: a collection of lectures by His Holiness the XIV Dalai Lama.* Thorsons Publishers.

Lazarus, K., & Rossouw, P. (2015). Mothers' expectations of parenthood: the impact of prenatal expectations on self-esteem, depression, anxiety and stress post birth. *International Journal of Neuropsychotherapy, 3*(2), 102-123. doi:10.12744/ijnpt.2015.0102-0123

Levine, A., & Heller, S. (2012). *Attached: the new science of adult attachment and how it can help you find and keep love.* New York: Penguin Random House.

MacBeth, A., & Gumley, A. (2012). Exploring compassion: a metaanalysis of the association between self-compassion and psychopathology. *Clinical Psychology Review, 32*(6), 545-552. doi:10.1016/j.cpr.2012.06.003

Moreira, H., Gouveia, M. J., Carona, C., Silva, N., & Canavarro, M. (2015). Maternal attachment and children's quality of life: the mediating role of self compassion and parenting stress. *Journal of Child and Family Studies, 24,* 2332-2344. doi:10.1007/s10826-014-0036-z

Neff, K. (2012). The science of self compassion. In C. Germer, & R. Siegel, *Compassion and Wisdom in Psychotherapy* (pp. 79-92). New York: Guilford Press.

Neff, K., & Costigan, A. (2014). Self-compassion, wellbeing and happiness. *Psychologie Osterreich, 2*(3), 114-119. Retrieved from http://self-compassion.org/wp-content/uploads/publications/Neff&Costigan.pdf

Neff, K., & Germer, C. (2012). A pilot study of randomized controlled trila of the Mindful Self-Compassion Program. *Journal of Clinical Psychology*. doi:10.1002/jclp.21923

Neff, K., Hsieh, Y., & Dejitterat, K. (2005). Self-compassion, achievement goals and coping with academic failure. *Self and Identity, 4*(3), 263-287. doi:10.1080/13576500444000317

PANDA. (2017). *PANDA*. Retrieved from Perinatal Anxiety and Depression Australia: https://www.panda.org.au

Pauley, G., & McPherson, S. (2010). The experience and meaning of compassion and self-compassion for individuals with depression or anxiety. *83*, 129-143. doi:10.1348/147608309X471000

Pawluski, J., Lonstein, J., & Fleming, A. (2017). The neurobiology of postpartum anxiety and depression. *Trends in Neuroscience, 40*(2), 106-119. Retrieved from http://dx.doi.org/10.1016/j.tins.2016.11.009

Poobalan, A., Aucott, L., Ross, L., Smith, W., Helms, P., & Williams, J. (2007). Effects of treating postnatal depression on mother-infant interaction and child development. *British Journal of Psychiatry, 191*, 378-386. doi:10.192/bjp.bp.106.032789

Poole Heller, D. (2015). *Dr. Diane Poole Heller*. Retrieved from Dr.Diane Poole Heller: https://dianepooleheller.com

Rockliff, H., Gilbert, P., McEwan, K., Lightman, S., & Glover, D. (2008). A pilot exploration of heart rate variability and salivary cortisol responses to compassion focused imagery. *Clinical Neuropsychiatry, 5*, 132-139.

Shapira, L., & Mongrain, M. (2010). The benefits of self compassion and optimism exercises for indviduals vulnerable to depression. *The Journal of Positive Psychology, 5*(5), 377-389. doi:10.1080/17439760.2010.516763

Siegel, D., & Sroufe, A. (2017). *The verdict is in: the case for attachment theory* . Siegel.

Smeets, E., Neff, K., Alberts, H., & Peters, M. (2014). Meeting suffering with kindess. Effects of a brief self compassion intervention for female college students. *Journal of Clinical Psychology*. doi:10.1002/jclp.22076

Swalm, D. (2015, October 13). *Women and Newborn Health Services*. Retrieved from King Edward Memorial Hospital: http://www.kemh.health.wa.gov.au/brochures/health_professionals/8393.pdf

Van Parys, H., Smith, J., & Rober, P. (2014). Growing up with a mother with depression: an Interpretative Phenomenological Analysis. *The Qualitative Report, 19*(29), 1-18. Retrieved from http://www.nova.edu.sss/QR/QR19/van_parys29.pdf

Wagstaff, C., Hyeseung, J., Nolan, M., Wilson, T., Tweedlie, J., Phillips, E., . . . Holland, F. (2014). The accordion and the deep bowl of spaghetti: eight researchers' experiences of using IPA as a methodology. *The Qualitative Report, 19*(47), 1-15. Retrieved from http://www.nova.edu.ssss/QR/QR19?wagstaff47.pdf

Walsh, R. (2011). Lifestyle and mental health. *American Psychological Association, 66*(7), 579-592.

Wardrop, A., & Popadiuk, N. (2013). Women's experiences with postpartum anxiety: Expectations, relationships and sociocultural influences. *The Qualitative Report, 18*, 1-24. Retrieved from http://www.nova.edu/ssss/QR/QR18/wardrop6.pdf

Wenzel, A., Huagen, E., Jackson, L., & Brendle, J. (2005). Anxiety symptoms and disorders at eight weeks postpartum. *Journal of Anxiety Disorders, 19*, 295-311. doi:10.1016/j.janxdis.2004.04.001

Yarnell, L., & Neff, K. (2012). Self-compassion, interpersonal conflict resolutions and wellbeing. *Self and Identity, 12*(2), 146-159. doi:10/1080/15298868.2011.649545

Yelland, J., Sutherland, G., & Brown, S. (2010). Postpartum anxiety, depression and social health: findings from a populations based survey of Australian women. *BMC Public Health, 10*, 771-781. doi:10.1186/1471-2458-10-771

About the Author

Cindy Cranswick was born and raised in Zimbabwe and immigrated to Perth in 2002. Growing up in Africa provided Cindy with a natural ability to be accepting and understanding of people of all cultures and set the stage for a colourful and varied life. Cindy has a loving family who have encouraged her and supported her to be her best self. She has two amazing daughters who she is very proud of and considers them to be her greatest achievements in life.

Cindy's working life started out in the IT world where she had many roles and many adventures for 25 years. After a marriage break-up in her early forties she decided to reinvent herself and went back to university to study counselling. Cindy has a private counselling practice where she offers counselling to individuals, couples and families. Cindy assists clients in the areas of anxiety, depression, relationship issues, sexuality, addictions, retirement transition, PNDA (Post Natal Depression and Anxiety), self-esteem and body image. Cindy has a number of years experience in women's health and wellbeing issues and has a special interest in PNDA counselling. Cindy is also a qualified clinical supervisor offering clinical supervision to other professionals in the industry as well as to students. She is a lecturer at the University of Notre Dame and a professional speaker. Cindy recently completed her Master of Philosophy and produced a thesis on her research findings into the role of self-compassion in the lives of women who experience anxiety and depression in the perinatal period.

Cindy is passionate about helping individuals acknowledge and accept the changes in their lives by empowering them with skills and knowledge to restore their sense of wellbeing. Cindy believes that although any form of change is a challenge to an individual, it is also an opportunity for growth.

Cindy Cranswick (M.Phil. B.Couns.)

info@changesforlife.com.au

www.changesforlife.com.au

SELF-COMPASSIONATE MOTHERHOOD PROGRAM

This program will take you on a journey of self-discovery and provide you with skills to bring the joy back into motherhood.

- Module 1 — Recreating Your Identity as a Mother
- Module 2 — Essential Ingredients for Motherhood
- Module 3 — Self-Acceptance and Self-Kindness
- Module 4 — Expectations and Being Human
- Module 5 — Emotions and Mindfulness
- Module 6 — Steps to Make Motherhood Meaningful

The program is based on the book "Self-compassionate Motherhood" and is designed for individuals or groups.

For more information please email info@changesforlife.com.au

www.changesforlife.com.au